JENNIE LOW'S SZECHUAN COOKBOOK

PRESIDIO

Published by Presidio Press, 31 Pamaron Way, Novato, CA 94947

Library of Congress Cataloging in Publication Data

Low, Jennie, 1940–
    Jennie Low's Szechuan cookbook.

    Includes index.
    1. Cookery, Chinese.   I. Title.
TX724.5.C5L68   1982   641.5951   82-9861
ISBN 0-89141-165-8

Cover design by Kathleen A. Jaeger
Illustrations by Suzie Taylor
Composition by Helen Epperson
Printed in the United States of America

I wish to dedicate this book to my many students, past and present. Their encouragement and support has enabled me to complete this project, which has occupied my every spare moment for the past two years.

It has not been, however, all drudgery. It has been a labor of love. My love for cooking, my love for teaching, and my love for the food of my ancestors are all part of this book.

A special thanks to my husband, John, for his invaluable assistance and moral support, and to my daughters Cindy and Denise, who assumed some of my chores. I am grateful to Lauan Garnjost for helping me put my thoughts into words and for typing the manuscript, and to Ailie Knorr and Doong Tien for their meticulous proofreading and suggestions. Others too gave of their talents to help create this book, and to all I say, ''Thank you.''

CONTENTS

INTRODUCTION

Each time I begin a new cooking class, I see before me a group of faces, each seeming to ask the same question: "Can I, too, cook Chinese?" I tell them this story. I arrived in America from Hong Kong 22 years ago. I spoke little English and, worse yet, did not know how to cook even one grain of rice. My uncle, with whom I stayed, was a master chef. Every week he spent his day off cooking marvelous foods for his family, and he would say to me, "Watch, now, so that you will know how to cook this yourself someday." Alas! Being young and carefree, I paid no heed. We would all sit down and enjoy the food to our hearts' content, then wash the dishes. My uncle would say, "Oh, Jennie! How are you ever going to learn how to cook?"

Then one day, I married, as young girls do, and my husband liked Chinese food like his mother used to make. What to do? My uncle was no longer around to show me. When I asked my Auntie, "How do you cook fish heads like his mother used to prepare them?" she would answer, "Ask his mother!" Of course, that I was reluctant to do. So then Auntie would tell me: "Chop the fish, give a sprinkle of this, a sprinkle of that, and you have it."

That is how I learned to cook—a sprinkle of this, a sprinkle of that. If it wasn't just right, next time I tried a bigger sprinkle of this and a smaller sprinkle of that, until I was satisfied with the recipe. Next, I carefully measured the exact amounts of each ingredient so that I could prepare a perfect dish each time. In this way, I developed a large number of recipes, many of which I have shared with my cooking classes for over 15 years. I call my method "home-style" cooking because I do not use monosodium glutamate (MSG); the flavor of the dishes and the tenderness of the meat come only from the food itself, the seasoning, and the marinades.

In 1974, I published *Chopsticks, Cleaver and Wok,* a compilation of many of these recipes, which is now in its sixth printing. This second collection of my own recipes follows the same step-by-step format that was so successful in my first cookbook.

The American taste in Chinese cuisine has become increasingly more sophisticated, craving the more exotic dishes from other provinces of China in addition to the many (and perhaps more familiar) dishes from Canton, the "kitchen province" of China. In this book, I have included recipes for many northern Chinese dishes and spicy Szechuan items, as well as dim sum delicacies, in order to meet this new demand.

Here, briefly, are descriptions of the different Chinese cuisines:

Cantonese cooking features mainly stir-fried or steamed dishes. The sauces are light but flavorful. This style of cuisine is the best known in the United States because most Chinese restaurants here were Cantonese until fairly recently. Cantonese dishes include shark's fin soup, chicken salad, steak cubes with Chinese greens, and seafood specialties, particularly steamed fish. Chow mein and a variety of foods cooked with black bean sauce are other favorites.

Mandarin cooking uses a great deal of sesame oil, wine, and wine vinegar. The dishes have more gravy than Cantonese dishes, and the wine-cooked meats are outstanding. Pan-frying is more common than stir-frying, and noodles are served more often than rice. Food is spicy, and hot oil (or chili oil) is used as a condiment. Hot and sour soup and sizzling rice soup are popular, as are mo shu pork with Mandarin pancakes and pot stickers. Other specialties are Mandarin crispy duck and Mandarin beef (sometimes called "Mongolian beef").

Szechuan cuisine is hot and spicy. It uses large amounts of chili pepper, Szechuan bean sauce, and chili sauce with garlic, and hot oil is always found on the table for use as a condiment. Garlic is an important seasoning and is used in generous amounts. Szechuan spiced chicken and garlic chicken are typical of Szechuan cuisine. Hot and sour beef, prawns a la Szechuan, and fish in hot bean sauce are also popular dishes. Eggplant is used in many Szechuan dishes. Hunanese cuisine is also piquant, but contains even more garlic than does Szechuan.

"Dim sum" (literally translated "touching the heart") is the Chinese Tea Lunch, the Cantonese version of the American brunch. A variety of steamed, deep-fried, braised, or baked delicacies, each one only a bite or two, are served with tea to make a delightful and satisfying meal. Many of the tea pastries (such as shrimp dumplings, half moon dumplings, pot stickers, won ton, and egg rolls) are made from special fillings wrapped in thin noodle skins, and each has a traditional shape to help identify it. In a tea house, these tidbits are served from trays or from carts wheeled past your table, in steam trays or on small plates. (An expensive item will have an extra plate under it.) At the end of the meal, the waiter merely adds up the plates and steam trays to calculate your check.

To enjoy the greatest variety of dim sum, go to a tea house with several friends. You may wish to order won ton soup, chow mein or chow fun, or a rice casserole in addition to the usual tea pastries. Discover your favorites, then use the recipes in this book to create them at home. (Most tea houses also sell some items "to go.")

ABOUT CHINESE COOKING

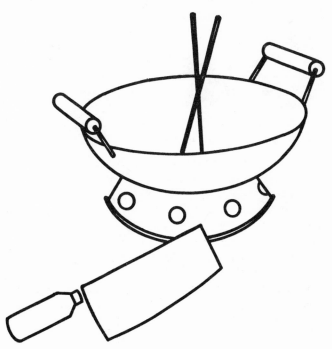

3. Invert pancake, sprinkle with ¼ tsp. salt, and pan-fry until golden brown (about 5 minutes). While still hot, break pancakes apart and remove to a bowl. Repeat procedure with remaining noodles.

4. Skin and bone chicken breast. Cut chicken into thin strips, julienne style. Sprinkle on seasoning and mix well.

5. Boil Chinese mushrooms in 1 cup warm water for 10 minutes. Rinse, drain, squeeze dry, and cut off and discard stem. Cut mushrooms into strips, julienne style.

6. Cut barbecued pork into thin strips, julienne style.

7. Using a vegetable peeler, remove tough outer layer of celery. Cut crosswise into 1½-inch pieces, then cut each piece lengthwise into strips, julienne style.

8. Heat wok and add 1½ tbsp. oil, chicken, and Chinese mushrooms. (If using fresh mushrooms, add with celery in step 9.) Stir-fry for 2 minutes over high heat. Add chicken stock. Cover and cook for 4 minutes.

9. Add barbecued pork, celery, bean sprouts, and green onion. Immediately sprinkle with ¼ tsp. salt and cook for 1 minute. Remove half of mixture and set aside.

10. Add half of pan-fried noodles to wok along with 1 tsp. oyster sauce and ½ tsp. thin soy sauce. Mix thoroughly (approximately 2 minutes). Remove to a platter and keep warm while repeating procedure with remaining noodles and meat mixture, oyster sauce and thin soy sauce. Serve.

Condiments: Serve with Hot Oil (page 54) or Hot Mustard (page 53).

Advance preparation: Steps 1 through 3 may be completed 3 days ahead and refrigerated. Steps 4 through 8 may be done a few hours in advance and kept at room temperature until you are ready to complete dish.

Serving suggestion: Serve for lunch, or use as a dish with others for dinner.

Note: Leftover chow mein can be refrigerated for several days and reheated without oil in a Teflon frying pan by stir-frying for several minutes.

*See Glossary, page 191.

NOODLE SOUP WITH BARBECUED PORK
叉燒湯麵

2 qt.	water		½ lb.	Napa cabbage
1 lb.	fresh Chinese noodles*		1½ qt.	chicken stock
½ lb.	Chinese Barbecued Pork, page 110		2	green onions, finely chopped

1. Bring 2 qt. water to a boil. Add noodles. Cook, uncovered, for 2 minutes. Pour into a colander and rinse with cold water. Drain and set aside.

2. Cut barbecued pork into ¼-inch-thick slices approximately 1½-by-½ inch.

3. Cut Napa cabbage into 1-inch pieces.

4. Bring chicken stock to a boil. Add Napa cabbage, cooked noodles, and barbecued pork. Cover and cook for 2 minutes.

5. Serve in individual bowls, garnished with chopped green onions.

Condiment: Serve small dishes containing a mixture of 1 tsp. thin soy sauce and 1 tsp. oyster sauce. Hot Mustard (page 53) or Hot Oil (page 54) may be used for a spicier taste.

Advance preparation: Steps 1 through 3 may be done the day before and refrigerated.

Serving suggestion: Serve for lunch or as a snack.

Variation: Cooked ham or chicken may be substituted for barbecued pork.

*See Glossary, page 191.

NOODLES WITH CHICKEN AND BAMBOO SHOOTS
鴻圖伊麵

2 qt.	water
½ lb.	deep-fried noodles*
½ lb.	chicken meat or pork butt (¾ cup diced)
¼ lb.	fresh mushrooms
¼ can	bamboo shoots** (approx. ½ cup diced)
4½ cups	chicken stock
1 tbsp.	oil
⅔ cup	chicken stock
¼ cup	frozen peas, defrosted
1	green onion, finely chopped

SEASONING

¼ tsp.	salt
¼ tsp.	sugar
½ tsp.	thin soy sauce
½ tsp.	oyster sauce
1 tsp.	white wine
1 tsp.	cornstarch
Dash	pepper

THICKENING MIXTURE

2½ tsp.	cornstarch mixed well with
2 tbsp.	cold water
1½ tsp.	dark soy sauce
2½ tsp.	sesame oil

1. Bring 2 qt. water to a boil. Add noodles. Cook, uncovered, for 2 minutes. Pour into a colander and rinse with cold water. Drain and set aside.

2. Cut chicken or pork, fresh mushrooms, and bamboo shoots into ⅓-inch cubes.

3. Sprinkle seasoning on chicken or pork and mix well.

4. Bring 4½ cups chicken stock to a boil. Meanwhile, heat wok. Add oil and chicken or pork. Stir-fry 2 minutes over high heat. Add bamboo shoots and ⅔ cup chicken stock. Cover and cook 2 minutes. Add peas and fresh mushrooms. Bring to a fast boil.

5. Stir in thickening mixture. Cook 30 seconds over high heat. Keep warm.

(continued)

6. Add noodles to boiling chicken stock (step 4) and cook for 1 minute. Pour into a large serving bowl. Top with meat and vegetable mixture from step 5. Garnish with chopped green onion. Serve.

Advance preparation: Steps 1 through 3 may be done a few hours ahead and kept at room temperature.

Serving suggestion: This soup can be served in 1 large serving bowl or in individual bowls with chicken-vegetable mixture topping and green onion garnish.

Variation: Fresh Chinese noodles may be substituted for deep-fried noodles. Use same cooking time.

*Deep-fried noodles are called "long life mein." See Glossary, page 190.

**See Glossary.

STIR-FRIED RICE NOODLES
肉絲炒粉

Serves 8

1 pkg.	rice sticks*	3 tsp.	dark soy sauce
2 qt.	water	3 tsp.	thin soy sauce
½ lb.	fresh pork butt	2 tbsp.	oyster sauce
5 tbsp.	oil	1½ tbsp.	sesame oil
½ lb.	cabbage, shredded	**SEASONING**	
1 lb.	bean sprouts, rinsed and drained	½ tsp.	salt
½ tsp.	salt (for vegetables)	½ tsp.	sugar
½ tsp.	sugar	1 tsp.	thin soy sauce
⅓ cup	chicken stock	1 tsp.	oyster sauce
1½ tsp.	salt	2 tsp.	cornstarch
½ lb.	Chinese Barbecued Pork, page 110, slivered		

1. Place rice sticks in a big bowl. Add warm water to cover. Soak for 30 minutes. Drain.

2. Bring 2 qt. water to a boil in a wok. Add rice sticks and boil for 1 minute. (Test for doneness by pinching a rice stick. If it breaks easily, it's cooked.) Drain. Rinse under cold water. Drain and set aside.

3. Cut pork butt into thin strips. Sprinkle on seasoning and mix well.

4. Heat wok. Add 1 tbsp. oil, cabbage, and bean sprouts. Stir-fry for 1½ minutes over high heat. Sprinkle with ½ tsp. salt and ½ tsp. sugar. Mix well, remove from wok, and set aside.

5. Heat wok. Add 1 tbsp. oil and seasoned pork. Stir-fry for 2 minutes over high heat. Add ⅓ cup chicken stock, cover, and cook 4 minutes. Remove to a large bowl and add cooked vegetables and barbecued pork. Set aside.

6. Rinse and stir rice sticks under cold water. Drain. (They must be slightly moist so they won't stick together when stir-fried.) Immediately heat wok. Add 1½ tbsp. oil and half of rice sticks. Stir-fry for 2 minutes over high heat. Add ¾ tsp. salt, 1½ tsp. dark soy sauce, 1½ tsp. thin soy sauce, 1 tbsp. oyster sauce, and ¾ tbsp. sesame oil. Mix thoroughly. Add half of meat and vegetable mixture. Mix well again (about 1 minute). Remove to a serving platter and keep warm. Repeat procedure with remaining noodles, meat, and vegetables. Serve.

Advance preparation: Steps 1 through 5 may be done a few hours ahead and kept at room temperature until you are ready to complete step 6.

Condiment: Serve with Hot Mustard, page 53.

Serving suggestion: You may wish to serve soy sauce as well as hot mustard with this dish. Serve for lunch or with other dishes for dinner.

*This dish calls for ¼-inch-wide rice sticks, which are preferred for stir-frying. Buy Lucky brand. See Glossary.

CHICKEN AND MUSHROOM RICE CASSEROLE
雞飯

15	small Chinese mushrooms (dried)
1 cup	warm water
3	dried red dates*
1½ lb.	chicken breasts or thighs (about 1½ cups chicken meat)
1 tbsp.	oil
1 tsp.	slivered ginger
1	green onion, slivered
3 cups	raw long-grain rice
2 cups	cold water
1	Chinese sausage, rinsed (optional)
1 tbsp.	dark soy sauce

SEASONING

1 tsp.	salt
1 tsp.	sugar
2 tsp.	white wine
2 tsp.	thin soy sauce
1 tbsp.	oyster sauce
1 tbsp.	cornstarch
1 tbsp.	cold water

THICKENING MIXTURE

½ tbsp.	cornstarch mixed well with
1 tbsp.	cold water

1. Boil mushrooms in 1 cup warm water for 10 minutes. Rinse, drain, and squeeze dry. Remove and discard stems. Cut mushrooms into thin strips, julienne style.

2. Rinse red dates. Remove and discard seeds. Cut dates into strips.

3. Skin and bone chicken breasts or thighs. Cut into ¼-inch-thick slices about 1½-by-1 inch. Sprinkle on seasoning and mix well.

4. Heat wok. Add 1 tbsp. oil, chicken meat, and mushrooms. Stir-fry for 2 minutes over high heat.

5. Stir in thickening mixture and cook for 30 seconds. Add red dates, slivered ginger, and slivered green onion. Set aside.

6. Place 3 cups rice in a 2½-qt. saucepan. (Do not use a rice cooker for this recipe—the rice and chicken will not cook properly.) Wash thoroughly 4 times. Drain off excess water. Add 2 cups cold water and Chinese sausage. Cover and cook over high heat for 7 minutes.

7. Add chicken mixture to rice. (There should still be water visible; otherwise chicken will not cook sufficiently.) Reduce heat to medium low. Simmer for 15–20 minutes. Remove Chinese sausage and slice it diagonally into about 10 thin slices. Set aside. Serve rice mixture in individual rice bowls. Sprinkle with a small amount of dark soy sauce. Place several slices of sausage on each portion.

Advance preparation: Steps 1 through 5 may be done a few hours ahead and kept at room temperature.

Serving suggestion: This dish is a complete meal in itself for lunch, or it may be served for dinner with 1 vegetable dish.

Note: This recipe is called a "casserole" because in a dim sum restaurant it is served in individual casseroles.

*See Glossary, page 193.

CURRY FRIED RICE
咖喱炒飯
Serves 6

2½ tbsp.	oil	½ cup	diced fresh mushrooms
3	eggs, lightly beaten with fork	1 cup	bean sprouts, washed and drained
1½ tsp.	curry powder	1 cup	shredded iceberg lettuce
1 recipe	Steamed Rice,* page 179, cooled (4 cups cooked rice)	1 tsp.	salt
		½ tbsp.	dark soy sauce
½ cup	diced Chinese Barbecued Pork, page 110	1 tbsp.	oyster sauce
1	green onion, finely chopped		

1. Heat wok. Add ½ tbsp. oil. Add eggs, scramble lightly; remove from wok and set aside.

2. Heat wok. Add 2 tbsp. oil, curry powder, and cool cooked rice. Stir-fry for 5 minutes over medium heat, breaking up lumps with a spatula. (If using leftover rice and rice is hard, add 2 tsp. water to soften it.)

3. Add barbecued pork, green onion, fresh mushrooms, and bean sprouts. Mix well (about 1 minute).

4. Add salt, dark soy sauce, and oyster sauce. Mix thoroughly.

(continued)

5. Add scrambled egg and iceberg lettuce. Mix well and serve.

Advance preparation: This recipe may be cooked in advance and reheated in a Teflon frying pan without oil for 1 minute.

Serving suggestion: Serve with any Chinese dish for lunch or dinner.

Variation: Cooked ham or cooked chicken may be substituted for barbecued pork.

Note: This dish will be a favorite with those who like curry, and possibly with some who think they don't care for it.

*Cook rice in advance and let it cool. Do not use freshly cooked hot rice: it will all stick together.

SHRIMP FRIED RICE
蝦仁炒飯

Serves 6

¼ lb.	(¾ cup) raw prawns in shells
3 tbsp.	oil
3	eggs, lightly beaten with a fork
2 strips	bacon
¼ cup	chopped yellow onion
1 recipe	Steamed Rice,* page 179 (4 cups cooked rice)
¼ lb.	bean sprouts (1 cup), washed and drained
2	green onions, finely chopped
1 tsp.	salt

½ tbsp.	dark soy sauce
1 tbsp.	oyster sauce

SEASONING

⅓ tsp.	salt
½ tsp.	thin soy sauce
1 tsp.	white wine
¾ tsp.	cornstarch
Dash	pepper

1. Shell, devein, wash, drain, and dice prawns into ¼-inch pieces.

2. Sprinkle on seasoning and mix well.

3. Heat wok. Add ½ tbsp. oil. Scramble eggs lightly; remove from wok and set aside.

4. Heat wok. Add ½ tbsp. oil. Cook bacon. Drain on paper towel. Chop fine.

178

5. Heat wok. Add 2 tbsp. oil. Stir-fry prawns and yellow onions for 30 seconds over medium heat. Add rice and stir-fry for 6 minutes. (If using leftover rice and rice is hard, add 2 tsp. of water to soften.)

6. Add bean sprouts, green onions, salt, dark soy sauce, oyster sauce, bacon, and scrambled egg. Mix thoroughly. Serve.

Advance preparation: This recipe may be cooked in advance and reheated in a Teflon frying pan without oil for 1 minute.

Serving suggestion: Serve fried rice with any Chinese dish for dinner, or as a 1-dish plate for lunch or dinner.

Variations: You may substitute cooked ham, Chinese barbecued pork, or cooked chicken for the bacon. You may substitute cooked shrimp for the prawns, adding it in step 6.

Note: Fried rice is the Chinese equivalent of Mulligan Stew. Almost any leftover food can be used in it.

*Cook rice in advance and let it cool. Do not use freshly cooked hot rice: it will stick together.

STEAMED RICE
白飯

Serves 4

2 cups   raw long-grain rice   3 cups   cold water

1. Put rice in a pot and wash it thoroughly 4 times in water. Drain off excess water.

2. Add cold water to rice, cover, and bring to a boil (it will take about 7–8 minutes at high heat).

3. Remove cover and continue cooking for about 5 minutes over high heat, until water is absorbed.

4. Cover and simmer for 10 minutes more over low flame. Be very careful at this point, as rice burns very easily. If rice is accidentally scorched, immediately remove from heat. It may be salvaged by placing a piece of bread in pot to absorb burnt flavor. (Discard bread.)

(continued)

Note: 1. Chinese have a unique way of measuring the amount of water used to prepare rice. If cooking 2 cups rice, they use a 2-qt. saucepan; if 3 cups, a 3-qt. saucepan. They add enough water to reach the first joint of a forefinger when it is just touching rice. Water level will then be just 1 inch above the surface of the rice. (When using an electric rice cooker, use only ¾ inch of water above rice, or follow directions provided with the cooker.)

2. Salt is never used when preparing steamed rice.

3. Chinese always wash rice 3 to 4 times before cooking.

4. If you use precooked packaged rice, follow directions on package.

5. One cup raw rice equals 2 cups cooked rice.

LIST OF INGREDIENTS

To aid the reader in shopping for the ingredients called for in this cookbook (and by special request of many of my students), I include the following glossary of ingredients. It will be helpful in identifying the various items found in Chinese grocery stores. I have also included the Chinese characters, which you need to know when seeking more unusual items. Bring the book with you when you shop.

BAMBOO SHOOTS
冬筍

Canned, packed in water. Look for "water packed," as there are also seasoned braised bamboo shoots. Companion brand is available in whole chunks or sliced. Ma Ling brand, which has recently become available, is good quality and reasonable in price. For best flavor, buy the chunks and slice your own. If possible, buy "winter bamboo shoots" (Companion brand). They are crisper and have a better flavor. To store, refrigerate in cold water in a covered container and change the water every 3 days. They will keep for 2 weeks.

BAMBOO SHOOT TIPS, DRIED
筍尖乾

Companion brand. Bamboo preserved in the dry form is used in the traditional New Year's dish, jai. It comes in 6-oz. boxes and will keep indefinitely at room temperature.

BEAN CAKES, FERMENTED (FURU)
腐乳

Quong Hop brand, sold in 16-oz. jars. Regular bean cakes that have been preserved through fermentation. Chinese use them as a simple accompaniment to steamed rice, flavored with a little sugar and eaten in small bits with a bite of rice. Also used in stir-fried vegetables, meats, and clams, and as flavoring with boiled chicken. Will keep well for up to 2 years under refrigeration because of the natural fermentation process.

BEAN CAKE, FRESH (TOFU)
豆腐

Fresh bean cake is found in plastic containers in the refrigerated section of the market. Brands commonly found are Azumaya and Wo Chong. There are two consistencies, soft and firm. Soft bean cake (usually packaged in one big chunk) is too soft for the recipes in this book. Use firm bean cake, which usually comes in two or four pieces. Bean cake is an excellent protein source, and although bland, it readily takes on other flavors. It should not be confused with "fermented bean cake," which comes in jars. Bean cake will keep in cold water in the refrigerator for 2 days.

BEAN CURD, DRIED SWEETENED
甜竹

Pearl River brand, from mainland China. Bean curd preserved by drying, used in the traditional New Year's dish, jai. It should not be confused with the unsweetened variety, which has more uses in Chinese cooking. Will keep indefinitely at room temperature.

BEAN CURD, WET
南乳

This is made from soybeans and red rice, and comes packed in brine in 8-oz. cans. Mee Chun brand is most common. This is not the same product as fresh bean cake (tofu) and the two should not be confused. Wet bean curd is used for flavoring, and only a small amount is used in a dish. It is used in jai, the vegetarian dish traditionally served at New Year's, and in the stewing of beef and duck. To store, remove from can to a covered jar and refrigerate. Keeps indefinitely.

BEAN SAUCES
豆瓣醬

The Sze Chuan Food Co. of Taiwan packages three different kinds of bean sauces. Each one is different and has different uses. Bean sauces will keep up to three years if removed from can to covered jar and refrigerated.

Bean Sauce
原豉醬

is the regular mixture, preferred for Cantonese-style cooking. This is also available in Koon Chun brand. There is also a "ground" bean sauce, but I don't recommend it for these recipes.

Hot Bean Sauce
辣豆瓣醬

has hot chili peppers added. This is the type used in Szechuan- and Northern-style cuisine.

Sweet Bean Sauce
甜麵醬

is used in cooking and as a condiment. It is sometimes served with peking duck or mo shu pork instead of hoisin sauce, but it does not replace hoisin sauce in cooking.

BEAN SPROUTS
芽菜

A unique and very tasty vegetable sprouted from beans. Fresh bean sprouts are firm and shiny. Do not buy limp, brownish sprouts. (Canned bean sprouts are available but are seldom satisfactory.) The bean sprouts found in supermarkets are from the small olive-green mung bean; the recipes in this book call for this type of sprout. These require almost no cooking and are delightful in stir-fried dishes combined with any meat, fowl, or fish. In Oriental grocery stores, you will also find sprouts from soy beans, which are larger than mung beans and yellow in color. These sprouts are larger, require longer cooking, and are therefore more often used in stewed dishes. The larger sprouts are generally unfamiliar to Occidentals. Each type of bean sprout has its own distinctive flavor. Stored in a plastic bag in the refrigerator, sprouts will keep about 2 days.

BEAN THREADS
粉絲

Bean threads (also called "cellophane noodles," "long rice," and "Chinese vermicelli") are made from mung bean starch. They look very similar to, and may be confused with, rice sticks (py mei fun), which are made from rice starch and water. Bean threads from Taiwan come wrapped in cellophane and take 12 minutes to cook. A brand now being imported from mainland China comes in a plastic bag, is finer than the Taiwan type, and requires only 6 minutes cooking time. Bean threads will keep indefinitely in a plastic bag in a dry place.

BITTER MELON
苦瓜

A shiny, light-green cucumber-shaped vegetable with a ridged and bumpy skin. As it really is bitter, due to quinine alkaloid, a taste for this vegetable must definitely be acquired. Some of the bitterness may be reduced by soaking in salt solution for 30 minutes, then parboiling. Bitter melon may be stuffed or stewed, or stir-fried with beef or chicken. Seasonal, from late May to August. Keeps 2 weeks refrigerated.

BLACK BEANS, SALTED (DOW SEE)
豆豉

There are two types of black beans. Hard beans come in plastic bags and are used in soups. The softer beans, which these recipes call for, also come in plastic bags, or in boxes, labeled "Salty Black Beans." These provide the delicious flavor in black bean sauce (sometimes called "lobster sauce" because it is the sauce served with Cantonese lobster). To make black bean sauce, the beans must first be rinsed twice to remove the excess salt. Do not bother to remove the "skin" that may wash loose. Place the beans in a bowl and mash them to a paste, along with a clove of minced garlic, using the butt of a cleaver. Black bean sauce is used with spareribs, steamed fish, prawns, and fresh crab and lobster. Keeps well for 2 years, refrigerated in a covered container.

BOK CHOY (CHINESE GREENS)
白菜

A popular vegetable in Chinese cooking, available the year around. Stir-fries nicely by itself, or with meats or fowl. The small tender shoots within the outer leaves are the best, similar to the hearts of lettuce. Choose bok choy of a smaller size for the best taste. Keeps 7–10 days under refrigeration.

CASHEW NUTS, RAW
腰果

These are sold in Oriental markets and health food stores. They will keep at room temperature for a few months, or up to 1 year when refrigerated. They can also be put in the freezer for 1–2 years.

CHICKEN STOCK
雞湯

To make your own, put a chicken carcass and a slice of ginger root in 2 qt. water. Bring slowly to a boil and simmer gently for 30 minutes. Add salt and dark soy sauce to taste, strain, and store in the refrigerator until ready to use. It will keep several days. Canned chicken broth, concentrated chicken base, or bouillon cubes may also be used.

CHILI PASTE WITH GARLIC
蒜蓉辣醬

Paste made from chili, salt, and garlic, and used to add spice to Szechuan dishes. Produced by Lan Chi Enterprises of Taiwan. Keeps well, refrigerated, for 2–3 years.

CHINESE BROCCOLI (GAI LON)
芥蘭

Green, like broccoli, and with a similar texture but fewer flowers. Very sweet and crunchy when stir-fried. The center stalk may be used but should first be stripped of its tough outer skin. Gai Lon is considered the king of vegetables by the Chinese gourmet. Available only in Chinese markets. Keeps 7–10 days refrigerated.

CHINESE PARSLEY
芫茜

Fresh coriander, also called cilantro in some markets. A small, delicate parsley that is very popular in Chinese cooking. It is used both for flavor and for visual appeal. It is a key ingredient in Chinese chicken salad and can be used to garnish any Chinese dish, especially noodles. Keeps 2 weeks under refrigeration; wash the parsley as you use it.

CHINESE SAUSAGE
臘腸

About the diameter of your thumb, 6 inches long, reddish in color. I recommend the pork sausage for most purposes, but beef and duck liver sausage are also available. It is sold prepackaged, but many Chinatown factories make their own, which are fresher and tastier. You'll see them in the shops, hanging by string, and you can buy any number you wish. Cook by steaming for 20 minutes, or add to the rice cooker with raw rice. Cut in pieces and serve, or chop and add to scrambled eggs. Uncooked sausages may be stored in the refrigerator for several months, or in the freezer for up to a year.

CORN EARS, BABY ("MINI-CORN")
玉米筍

Already cooked from the canning process, these are used in stir-fries, stews, and soups. Leftover corn will keep up to 2 weeks if rinsed and stored in cold water in a covered container in the refrigerator; change the water every 3 days.

CORNSTARCH
豆粉

Used in marinades to keep texture smooth, in batters for deep-frying, and as a thickener for gravies. Tapioca starch can be used as a substitute in most recipes. It will keep indefinitely in a dry place.

186

CURRY POWDER
咖喱

Many brands are available, but Madras most approximates the flavor I seek in all of my curry recipes. Madras is available in smaller tins. Curry powder keeps indefinitely at room temperature.

DUCK EGGS, SALTED
鹹蛋

Not to be confused with "thousand-year-old eggs." Salting is an ancient method of preserving, and the process changes the character of the egg. When hard-boiled, the egg white is firm and very salty, and the yolk gains a distinctive flavor from the rich oil developed in the salting process. The hard-boiled eggs are eaten with rice. The yolks alone are used raw in steamed pork cakes and as the symbolic "moon" in moon cakes. They are also used in "Chinese tamales" (joong): mixed with rice and pork, wrapped in ti leaves, and cooked for 5 hours. Both local and imported eggs are available. The imported eggs may be covered with a layer of clay (as are "thousand-year-old eggs").

DUCK EGGS, "THOUSAND-YEAR-OLD"
皮蛋

These eggs are not really that old! They are preserved with calcium salts (lime). The preserving process solidifies the egg into a gelatinous mixture, the egg white becoming a transparent greenish color and the yolk a green-gray semiliquid. They need no cooking. It is best to have some guidance upon introduction to this egg, since "bad eggs" turn up more than occasionally. Once the taste is acquired, the "thousand-year-old" egg is truly a gourmet treat! These eggs are often eaten with preserved sweet-and-sour ginger, with first a bite of egg, then a tiny bite of ginger. The combination of flavors is very pleasing. A word of caution when shopping: these eggs are encased in clay and may easily be confused with their salted cousins.

DUMPLING SKINS
燒賣皮

Sometimes these packages are labeled "dumpling skins," sometimes "siu mai skins," and sometimes they're not labeled at all. The skins are 3 inches in diameter and are similar in appearance to pot sticker skins but much thinner. There are 85 skins to each package, so the packages are thicker. Stored in a plastic bag in the refrigerator they will keep for 1 week, or in the freezer for 2 months. When frozen, thaw at least 5 hours at room temperature before using.

EGGPLANT, ORIENTAL
茄子

A purple-skinned vegetable about 6 inches long and 1½ inch thick, shaped somewhat like a crookneck squash. It is picked younger than regular eggplant and is therefore more tender. It is sometimes found in supermarkets but is usually available in Oriental markets. Refrigerated, it will keep about 2 weeks. If Oriental eggplant is not available, substitute eggplant.

EGG ROLL SKINS
春捲皮

These skins are about 6 inches square and come in 1-lb. packages. Recently, a thinner egg roll skin has become available. Because they are so thin, it takes a little more care to separate them for use, but a crispier egg roll makes it worth the effort. There are approximately 25 skins in a package. Look for the thinner product under the brand names Ho Tai, Menlo, Chinese Inn, or Doll. Leftover skins may be placed in a plastic bag and stored for a week in the refrigerator, or they may be frozen for 2 months. Be sure to thaw frozen skins for at least 5 hours at room temperature before using.

FIVE-SPICE POWDER
五香粉

A blend of ground fennel seed, star anise, cinnamon, black pepper, and cloves. It may be found in Oriental grocery stores in 2-oz. cellophane packages and is so inexpensive that it is easier to buy than to make it yourself. It will keep indefinitely in a closed jar in a dry place.

FUNGUS, DRIED BLACK (WOOD EARS)
木耳

A fungus used in mo shu pork, hot and sour soup, and stir-fried and steamed dishes. It is rather tasteless but lends texture and crispness to a dish. Very popular in northern Chinese cooking. It comes in a plastic bag and will keep at room temperature for 2–3 years.

FUNGUS, DRIED WHITE
雪耳

A light brown fungus, not to be confused with the more common black fungus. This fungus is used for soups only, whereas black fungus has a greater variety of uses. Packaged in a plastic box by Chong Chaen Company and by the People's Republic of China as "White Fungus Health Food." It will keep at room temperature for 2–3 years.

FUZZY MELON (MOH GWA)
毛瓜

A delicious melon, seasonal from late May through August, used to make soup, or stir-fried with meats or dried shrimp. It is like squash, light green in color, and not really hairy, but with tiny bristles, which are removed by paring off the skin. Avoid the larger sizes, which tend to be older and less tender; choose melons about 3 inches in diameter and 5 inches long. Store refrigerated for up to 2 weeks.

GARLIC
蒜子

Buy loose garlic rather than bagged garlic because the bud is larger and so are the cloves. To peel quickly, place a clove on a chopping board. Use the flat side of a cleaver (with the blade turned away from you!) to crush the garlic slightly, then simply peel away the loosened skin. Whole garlic keeps at room temperature for months.

GINGER, FRESH (GINGER ROOT)
薑

Available in many supermarkets and in any Oriental grocery, fresh ginger has a pleasant aroma and flavor and is much superior to ginger powder. You need not purchase a whole root—just snap off a portion. It will keep in a cool, dry place for several months. Do not wash more than you plan to use at one time (ginger will keep longer if kept dry). Peel before using. You may wish to peel a large piece of ginger and keep it in a jar of white wine, to avoid last-minute peeling.

GLUTINOUS RICE POWDER
糯米粉

Made from glutinous rice. Used in many dim sum dishes for its distinctive rice flavor. It is sticky when moistened and somewhat difficult to work with. Keeps well at room temperature for 2 years.

HOISIN SAUCE
海鮮醬

Made from sugar, vinegar, soybeans, fermented rice, chili, and spices, it is reddish-brown in color and slightly sweet. Hoisin sauce is used to flavor certain dishes and as a condiment with Peking duck and mo shu pork. The common brand is Koon Chun brand, which comes in a 16-oz. can. To store, place in a jar in the refrigerator. It will keep 2 years.

JICAMA
蕃葛

This vegetable, turnip shaped with a brown skin, is sweet and crispy and may be substituted for water chestnuts in stir-fried dishes or eaten raw like an apple. It is found in many grocery stores. Peel and slice only what you plan to use immediately. Refrigerate the remainder in a plastic bag with the top open. It will keep for several weeks.

LILY FLOWERS, DRIED (GOLDEN NEEDLE)
金針

Lily flowers usually come in 4-oz. packages, although some stores repackage them in 1-oz. sizes. (Packages are usually not labeled. If in doubt, ask!) Usually found near the dried mushrooms in a Chinese grocery store, they are about 3 inches long, less than ¼ inch wide, and golden in color (hence the name). Very inexpensive and an excellent source of protein. Soak in warm water for 10 minutes, then cut ¼ inch off the pointed ends (this part is tough). They will keep 2–3 years in a dry place.

LONG BEANS, CHINESE
青豆

These beans are about 2 feet long and come tied in bundles. They are seasonal, available from May to September. There is no waste because the entire bean is used, except the two tip ends. They are delightful stir-fried and will keep, refrigerated, for about 2 weeks.

MUSHROOMS, CHINESE (BLACK MUSHROOMS)
冬菇

One of the gourmet mushrooms and very expensive. Prices vary, depending on size. Since most recipes call for chopped mushrooms, it is not necessary to buy the larger, more expensive size except when serving black mushrooms as a dish by themselves. They are dried and very lightweight, so a pound is a lot. They will keep up to 2 years refrigerated.

MUSHROOMS, STRAW
草菇

These come in 15-oz. cans. Buy the ones labeled "peeled." Similar to button mushrooms, they are not expensive and cook very quickly. To store after opening, drain, place in a covered jar in cold water, and refrigerate. The water should be changed every 3 days. Straw mushrooms will keep up to 10 days stored this way.

MUSTARD GREENS, CHINESE
芥菜

A unique Chinese vegetable, usually available only in Chinese markets and not to be confused with the mustard greens found in supermarkets. Very good for making soup, but the flavor is not good for stir-frying. They will keep in the refrigerator for 2 weeks.

MUSTARD POWDER (DRY MUSTARD)
芥辣

Available in Chinese grocery stores, or use Coleman brand dry mustard. Mix thoroughly equal parts of powder and cold water to make hot mustard, which is used as a condiment with many dishes. It keeps indefinitely.

NAPA CABBAGE (CHINESE CABBAGE)
紹菜

A year-round vegetable, not to be confused with bok choy. It has stalks similar to celery, with crinkly yellowish-white leaves. Both the leaves and the entire stalk are used, so there is no waste. It stir-fries nicely with meats or fowl and is also very good in soup. Refrigerated, it will keep up to 2 weeks.

NOODLES, DEEP-FRIED
長壽麵

These noodles are already deep-fried and come pressed into ½-lb. "cakes" about 8 inches in diameter and 2 inches thick. They are also called "yee mein" or "long life mein," and are often served at birthday parties for good luck. (*Mein* means noodles, so whenever you see "mein" on a Chinese menu, you'll know it's a noodle dish.) Stored at room temperature, they will keep about 2 weeks. Do not confuse these noodles with the loose deep-fried noodles that resemble shoestring potatoes and are eaten "as is." Yee mein must be parboiled before serving.

NOODLES, FRESH CHINESE
麵

Fresh Chinese noodles are made in different widths and are sold in 1-lb. plastic bags. The ¼-inch-wide noodles are used in soup. The fine noodles, called "egg noodles," are also used in soup and in lo mein (noodles in oyster sauce). For pan-fried noodles, buy the medium width. If in doubt, ask the grocery clerk. Fresh noodles will keep for 1 week in the refrigerator, or 2 months in the freezer. Thaw frozen noodles for several hours at room temperature before using.

OIL
油

Any good vegetable oil, such as safflower, peanut, corn, or cottonseed oil, may be used for Chinese cooking. Some cooks favor peanut oil, especially for deep-frying, but it is more expensive.

OIL, HOT

(Also called chili oil or hot pepper oil.) Found on the table in restaurants for use as a condiment, this oil is, as the name indicates, very spicy, and should be used cautiously at first by the uninitiated. It is available bottled, in Oriental food stores. However, I prefer the homemade version (see instructions on page 54), using safflower oil, which is lighter and more delicately flavored, with no unpleasant "greasy" aftertaste.

OYSTERS, DRIED
蠔豉

Oysters preserved by drying. Very expensive. Used sparingly in oyster toss, congee, and stews. Dried oysters usually come in cellophane packages, often unlabeled. They will keep 2 years if refrigerated.

OYSTER SAUCE
蠔油

A sauce made from oysters, salt, starch, and caramel coloring. It has a distinctive flavor (not fishy, if you buy a quality brand) and may be used in cooking or as a condiment. The more expensive brands (about $3) such as Hop Sing Lung or Lee Kum Kee, both from Hong Kong, are definitely superior in flavor and worth the extra expense. You may find two different labels (and two different prices) for the Lee Kum Kee brand. The "lady and child in a boat" label has been manufactured for many years, is only slightly more expensive than their newer red and white label, and is better. Oyster sauce will keep up to 2 years if refrigerated.

PEANUTS, RAW
花生

These are sold shelled and skinned in Oriental markets and in health food stores. Don't buy unskinned ones—it is too time-consuming to remove the skins yourself. Refrigerated, they will keep up to 1 year, or for a few months at room temperature.

PEPPERS, DRIED RED CHILI
乾辣椒

These come whole or crushed; recipes will specify which form to use. Used frequently in Szechuan- and northern-style cooking. They can be purchased in any supermarket and will keep indefinitely at room temperature.

PLUM SAUCE
蘇梅醬

Koon Chun brand yellow plum sauce, made from plums, sugar, vinegar, chili, and garlic. (Not the same as hoisin sauce.) Used as a condiment with roast duck and fried squid. To store, remove to a covered jar and refrigerate for up to 2 years.

PORK, BARBECUED
叉燒

Used in many recipes and as a garnish, it is delightful sliced and served cold with a dipping sauce. Relatively simple to make at home, it may also be purchased at Chinese delicatessens and at some markets in Chinatown for about $3 per pound (one need not buy a full pound). It will keep in the refrigerator for one week or for three months in the freezer.

PORK, GROUND

Do not buy prepackaged ground pork or "sausage meat" for use in these recipes; the meat contains too much fat. Buy pork butt (also called "Boston butt" or "pork shoulder"). Have your butcher trim off the fat and grind the meat, or grind it yourself in your food processor. You will have about 2 lb. ground meat. Wrap and freeze any extra ground pork.

POT STICKER SKINS
鍋貼皮

Made especially for pot stickers, these 3-inch-diameter skins come 40 skins to a package. They are labeled "Pot Sticker Skins" and should not be confused with dumpling skins, which are similar in size and appearance but much thinner. They will keep 1 week in a plastic bag in the refrigerator, or 2 months in the freezer. Thaw frozen skins for at least 5 hours at room temperature before using.

PRESERVED VEGETABLES, TIENTSIN BRAND
天津冬菜

Cabbage preserved with garlic and salt, packaged in a clay pot. Used for flavor in pot stickers, steamed fish, pork cake, and other dishes. Cover the top with aluminum foil and store in the refrigerator for up to 2 years.

RADISH, PRESERVED 榨菜	A Chinese radish preserved with chili powder, salt and spices, also labeled "preserved vegetable." I recommend Szechuan brand. Used to flavor steamed pork, to stir-fry, and in soups and noodle dishes. To store, remove from can to a closed jar and refrigerate for up to 2 years.
RED DATES, DRIED 紅棗	Small red dates, preserved by drying. Used for their natural sweetness in soups, steamed fish, and steamed chicken dishes. Store in a covered container in the refrigerator for up to 2 years.
RICE 米	Rice should be washed in cold water four times before cooking. All types of rice will keep for a year at room temperature in a dry place.
Long-grain Rice	Chinese people prefer long-grain rice. When properly cooked, each grain stays separate. Common brands available at Oriental markets are AA and Dynasty. Any brand from the supermarket may be used.
Short-grain Rice	This is slightly stickier than long-grain rice and is preferred by the Japanese. It is used for making the rice patties for sizzling rice soup and sizzling rice chicken. Whenever you see "Calrose" on a package, you will know it is short-grain rice. Popular brands are Shira Kiku and Hinode.
Sweet Rice 糯米	is too sweet to eat every day but is used in "Chinese tamales" (joong), eight precious pudding, and sweet rice rolls. When cooked, it has a shiny appearance. The only brand available is Sho Chiku-Bai, found in Oriental food markets.
RICE STICKS	Rice sticks are a dry noodle made from rice flour. They have a blander flavor than noodles and are preferred over noodles by the older generation of Chinese. There are two types:
Dried Rice Sticks	are ¼-inch wide and are used in stir-frying (chow fun) or are boiled and used in soup. They come in 1-lb. plastic bags, labeled "Lucky Brand Rice Sticks." Other brands are now also available. They store well and will keep 1 to 2 years at room temperature.
Py Mei Fun 排米粉	are fine and threadlike and may easily be confused with bean threads. They are imported from Hong Kong, Taiwan, Thailand, and Singapore and come in 1-lb. plastic bags or in parchmentlike wrappings. They are used for stir-fried dishes such as Singapore-style chow fun and for deep-frying. Deep-fried, they may be eaten as a snack, or they may be

used to add texture to a dish such as Cantonese chicken salad or Mongolian lamb. For deep-frying, buy the rice sticks in the parchment wrapper (they deep-fry better). When deep-frying rice sticks, the oil must be hot (350°). Test the oil temperature by dropping in a piece of rice stick; if it doesn't puff up immediately, the oil is not hot enough. Deep-fried rice sticks will keep for several days in an airtight container. Uncooked rice sticks will keep 1 to 2 years stored in a plastic bag at room temperature.

RICE VINEGAR, JAPANESE
醋

A mild, pleasant-tasting vinegar, preferred over the stronger cider vinegar for use in some dishes. (Also favored by many for use in salad dressings and other non-Oriental foods.) Fujita Brewing Company markets their vinegar in 24-oz. bottles only; Marukan vinegar comes in both 12.7-oz. and 25.4-oz. sizes. There are two types of Marukan vinegar, the "Genuine Brewed" (green label) and the "Seasoned Gourmet" (orange label). The latter contains salt, sugar, MSG, and caramel coloring. For the recipes in this book, I suggest you use the unseasoned (green label) type. Rice vinegar keeps indefinitely at room temperature.

ROASTING SALT
燒鹽

Used in roasting or barbecuing pork to give the meat its bright, reddish color and to enhance flavor. It may be purchased at Oriental grocery stores and is sometimes labeled "Curing Salt." It is very inexpensive and only a small amount is used. It keeps indefinitely in a dry place.

SALTED FISH (HOM YEU)
鹹魚

Included here for the benefit of my Chinese readers, although the more adventurous gourmet may wish to try it. A very pungent but tasty fish, preserved in the time-honored way by salting and sun-drying. Sold as a whole dried fish, it is used as an accompaniment to rice, or, more often, cooked with steamed pork cake. Adjust the seasoning of the latter to allow for the saltiness of the fish. A little bit goes a long way. To store, chop into 2-inch pieces, place in a covered container in sufficient vegetable oil to cover, and refrigerate. It will keep this way for 2 years. There are many varieties of salted fish, but Lee Soon Wak brand seems to have fewer bones. It may be difficult to find in local markets, but it is available in Chinese markets and is worth the search.

SCALLOPS, DRIED
江瑤柱

Very expensive, but very good! Dried scallops cost $40 per pound, but they may be purchased by the ounce. The bigger the scallop, the more costly. Use in soups, or shred and stir-fry with eggs. They will keep well for 2 years, refrigerated in a covered container.

SEAWEED, DRIED
紫菜

Dried seaweed comes in 2-oz. cellophane packages, sometimes not labeled. Until recently imported only from Japan, it now is imported from China also; one Chinese brand is labeled "Dried Laver." It will keep indefinitely at room temperature if stored in a dry place.

SESAME OIL
芝麻油

An oil pressed from sesame seeds, with a delightful but strong flavor. Use sparingly. It is used as a seasoning in many dishes, especially in Mandarin and Szechuan dishes, and is also used as a condiment. Buy sesame oil in an Oriental store or the Oriental section of the supermarket. It comes in 6-oz. and 16-oz. bottles; the brands most often found are Lucky and Sona. After opening, refrigerate sesame oil to prevent it from becoming rancid. If refrigerated, it will keep for 2 years or more. (When chilled, it solidifies slightly, but this will not affect its use in cooking. If using as a condiment, pour out the amount needed and let stand at room temperature for 2 hours.)

SESAME SEEDS
芝麻

There are white sesame seeds, which are the kind to be used in these recipes, and black sesame seeds, which are used to make a sweet pudding. Buy in bulk at an Oriental grocery or at a health food store. They will keep for a few months in an airtight container at room temperature. I recommend buying raw sesame seeds and toasting them yourself for freshest flavor.

SHRIMP, DRIED
蝦米

Sold in 4-oz. packages. Dried shrimp are expensive, but not as expensive as dried scallops. They can be rinsed and eaten as is, or used to flavor dishes such as soups and meat cakes. They will keep well in a covered container in the refrigerator for up to 2 years.

SNOW PEAS
蘭豆

Sometimes called "sugar peas" or "Chinese pea pods," this sweet and crunchy vegetable is everyone's favorite Chinese vegetable and is now available in most supermarkets. The flat pea pods are picked before the peas mature, and the entire pod is eaten. They add color and flavor to any dish. The Chinese hand pick snow peas one by one to get them when they are small and tender. They will keep in a plastic bag in the refrigerator for 2 weeks.

SOY SAUCE
豉油

A sauce made from soybean extract, wheat flour, salt, and water; used as a flavoring and as a condiment. In Chinese restaurants you may be served either thin soy sauce or dark soy sauce as a condiment, depending on the choice of the management. Brands commonly found are Koon Chun and Golden Label, both from Hong Kong, and Pearl River Bridge, now being imported from mainland China. After opening, soy sauce will keep at room temperature for many months, or in the refrigerator for 2 or more years.

Dark Soy Sauce
老抽

Sometimes called "black" soy sauce, dark soy sauce contains sugar in addition to the other ingredients and as a result has a more syrupy consistency and a less-salty flavor than thin soy sauce. Pearl River Bridge brand dark soy sauce is labeled "Soy, Superior Sauce." (Be careful: Pearl River Bridge thin and dark soy sauce bottles are almost identical; one way to tell the difference is to tip the bottle—dark soy will cling to the side of the bottle longer than thin soy.)

Thin Soy Sauce
生抽

Sometimes called "light" soy sauce. Lighter in color, saltier in flavor, and thinner than dark soy sauce. Pearl River Bridge brand thin soy sauce is labeled "Superior Soy."

SQUID, DRIED
金錢魷

Quite different in taste and texture from fresh squid. Used for its flavor, it is stronger than dried shrimp. It is sold in 8-oz. plastic packages and keeps for up to 1 year at room temperature.

STAR ANISE
八角

A star-shaped seed pod that imparts a licorice flavor to stews. One of the elements of five-spice powder, it comes in 2-oz. cellophane packages. The whole spice has 5 or 6 points but in packages is quite often broken, so you may have to estimate the number of pieces equivalent to 1 whole pod. It will keep indefinitely in a closed jar in a dry place.

SUEY GOW SKINS
水餃皮

These skins are round, about 4 inches in diameter, and come approximately 60 to a package, wrapped in parchment paper. Do not confuse with dumpling skins (siu mai skins), which are considerably thinner. Stored in a plastic bag, they will keep for 1 week in the refrigerator or may be frozen for 2 months. Before using frozen skins, defrost at least 5 hours at room temperature.

TANGERINE PEEL
菓皮

The peel of the mandarin orange, tangerine, or tangelo, preserved by drying. Sometimes labeled "Orange Peel," it is imported from Hong Kong and comes in 1-oz. packages. It is used to flavor soups, stews, and steamed fish. It keeps indefinitely in a cool, dry place.

TAPIOCA STARCH (TAPIOCA POWDER)
菱粉

The dry starch is smooth like cornstarch and may be used instead of cornstarch in any recipe: it makes a slightly thicker sauce. In China, tapioca starch is used extensively for thickening since cornstarch is not available. It is used today in many Chinese restaurants in the United States. Store in a dry place at room temperature. It will keep for 2 or more years.

WATER CHESTNUTS
馬蹄

Fresh water chestnuts are imported from Taiwan and Hong Kong and are available in Chinese markets. They are delightful eaten raw, with a sweetness and texture reminiscent of apples. When added to won ton filling, meat cakes, or stir-fried vegetables, they give flavor and a crunchy texture. Use a sharp knife to slice off the top and bottom, then a vegetable peeler to remove the skin. Rinse and soak in cold water to prevent discoloring. They will keep in refrigerator for a couple of days. Unpeeled, they will keep 2 weeks, refrigerated. Jicama may be substituted (see "Jicama").

Canned water chestnuts are already peeled, and the canning process softens them somewhat. They are not as crisp or as flavorful as the fresh ones, but they still give texture to stir-fried dishes. Their taste may be improved by stir-frying in a little oil and adding a small amount of sugar before using in a recipe. They will keep refrigerated, in water, for 2 weeks. Change the water every 3 days.

WATER CHESTNUT POWDER (WATER CHESTNUT STARCH)
馬蹄粉

This has a somewhat grainy texture compared to cornstarch. It comes in 8-oz. boxes and may be found in Oriental markets. The most common brands are Companion and Chi Kong. Stored in a dry place at room temperature, it will keep indefinitely.

WHEAT STARCH
澄麵粉

A starch made from wheat, somewhat resembling cornstarch. Used for making dough for dim sum dishes such as pork dumplings, shrimp dumplings, and half-moon dumplings. Yue Yuen Loon and Foo Lung Ching Kee brands are the ones most commonly found. It will keep 2 years at room temperature in a dry place.

WINE, RICE
紹興酒

Used in some stir-fry cooking. Any type of rice wine may be used, such as Japanese rice wine or Shao Hsing wine from Taiwan. Rice wine to be used for cooking will keep without refrigeration. Dry sauterne or dry sherry may be substituted, but it should be refrigerated.

WON TON SKINS
雲吞皮

These skins, 3½ inches square, come in 1-lb. packages (about 80 skins). They will keep in a plastic bag in the refrigerator for 1 week, or they may be frozen for 2 months. When frozen, thaw at least 5 hours at room temperature before using.

198

INDEX

COOKING UTENSILS

THE WOK

The wok is the primary utensil in the Chinese kitchen, used for stir-frying, deep-frying, pan-frying, steam cooking, and stewing. Its main advantage is its versatility. The wok can be used in much of your everyday cooking: for cooking bacon without splatter and spaghetti with no spilling over, or for deep-frying doughnuts and fritters with less oil. The shape of the wok permits cooking either a very small amount of food or a large amount with equal facility.

WHICH WOK TO BUY Woks come in all sizes and in many styles but only one shape: wok shape. They are available in 12-, 14-, and 16-inch diameters, and even larger. The most common size for the average home kitchen is the 12-inch or 14-inch wok.

The original wok had a round bottom and two handles. Modern woks come with either round or flat bottoms. Flat-bottomed woks do not need stands and sit well on electric stoves. The round-bottomed wok with a stand is a better choice for use on gas stoves. Stainless steel woks with copper bottoms, Teflon-coated woks, and electric woks are now available. I recommend a steel wok, or a stainless steel wok with copper bottom; these heat faster and hotter than woks made of other materials. The traditional two-handled wok allows the cook to pick up a heavy wok, laden with food, with two hands. Flat-bottomed woks come also with a single long handle.

CARE OF THE WOK Modern woks (stainless steel, Teflon, electric) need only be washed and air dried. Iron and steel woks, however, must be "seasoned" before using. To season a wok, pour 1 cup of vegetable oil into the wok (you may use "old" oil that has been used for cooking). Heat the wok over medium-low heat for 15 minutes, stirring the oil and coating the entire wok all the while. Discard the oil. Wipe the wok clean with a paper towel, then wash with soap and water. Instead of wiping dry, place the wok over a medium flame and heat dry. It is neces-

3

sary to do the oil heating only once. This will keep rust stains from forming. For the next 20 or more uses, heat dry after each cleaning. The wok will then be thoroughly seasoned, with the pores of the iron impregnated with oil. Thereafter, it may be wiped dry, without fear of rust spots forming.

THE CLEAVER

The second most important tool in the Chinese kitchen is the cleaver. It too is most versatile. The Chinese chef does almost all cutting with one or two cleavers: a light one for cutting and paring, a heavier one for chopping. (For home use, one lightweight cleaver is sufficient.) The flat of the blade is used to crush garlic or ginger, and as a spatula to pick up and transport chopped and minced foods. The butt of the cleaver is used as a pestle to mash black beans or bean sauce into a paste. Boning a chicken is much easier with a cleaver because the blade is heavier and wider.

Develop confidence with the cleaver by first using it to cut large items, such as bread, watermelon, and squash. (You can exert additional force by pressing on the back of the blade with your free hand.) You will soon discover the "feel" and the balance of the cleaver. In time, your ability will increase to the point where you can fine cut vegetables and meats as Chinese chefs do.

WHICH CLEAVER TO BUY
Like woks, cleavers come in different styles and different weights. They are usually made of fine steel. The handle may be of steel also, molded into one piece with the blade, or of wood, attached to the blade. The steel-handled cleaver is heavier but will never detach from the blade. The wooden handle gives a warmer feel, but it cannot be soaked in water or it will split. The most comfortable weight and size of cleaver for the home kitchen is the No. 3 weight. This size is sufficient for all home-style cooking.

CARE OF THE CLEAVER
The cleaver should be washed by hand and wiped dry immediately, to prevent rust spots. Do not wash it in the dishwasher. To sharpen, use a hand sharpener, a whetstone, a sharpening steel, or an electric sharpener.

CHINESE SPATULA

The Chinese spatula is made of stainless steel (preferably) or steel and is better suited for heavy use than ordinary household spatulas. The angle and shape of the blade are especially designed to fit the shape of the wok. Chinese spatulas are suited for stir-frying and for breaking up large pieces of food in the wok. Cold leftover rice, for example, may be broken up with the spatula while it is being stir-fried.

CHINESE STRAINER

The wide, flat wire strainer with a bamboo handle is another useful implement. The most common size is 6 inches in diameter. It can double as a colander, it is used to scoop noodles or other foods out of boiling water, and it is indispensable when deep-frying foods such as won tons, egg rolls, chicken, and potatoes. When deep-frying cashews, almonds, or peanuts, place them in a Chinese strainer so you can remove them from the oil quickly when they reach the desired golden-brown color.

STEAMERS

There are two kinds of steamers, aluminum and bamboo. The aluminum steamer is complete in itself, with a bottom compartment to hold water, two perforated steaming sections, and a cover. The bamboo steamer is used in the wok, with the wok holding the water. With this type of steamer, two layers of food may be steamed at one time. Bamboo steamers come in different diameters, the size being determined by the diameter of your wok.

You can also purchase an inexpensive steam plate to fit in your wok. An 11-inch size will fit most woks. I recommend an aluminum steam plate, although wooden stands are also available.

COOKING METHODS

STIR-FRYING

Stir-frying, developed centuries ago to conserve fuel, is the method most often used in Chinese cooking. Vegetables cooked this way retain their crispness, flavor, and natural color, and most important, their nutrients, because they are cooked so quickly. (*Chow* is the Chinese word for "stir-fry," so when you see it used as a prefix for a dish on a Chinese menu, you will know immediately that the dish is stir-fried.)

Temperature control is critical. A "feel" for the correct temperature will come with experience. The wok should be neither too hot (the food will burn) nor too cold (the food will stick). A stainless steel wok will heat in 30 seconds, a steel wok will take over a minute. *Never* add oil to a cold wok (or electric wok, or frying pan). The oil may never reach a temperature high enough to keep the food from sticking.

Please note: when you read "heat wok" in this cookbook, it means you should always start with a clean wok. If you have just used the wok for a previous step in the recipe, rinse it out well in hot water and wipe dry. Then heat the wok and proceed with the recipe.

When the wok is hot, add the oil in a circular motion and swirl the wok, or use your Chinese spatula, to coat the wok thoroughly. Add food immediately (it should sizzle if the wok is hot enough) and stir back and forth with the inverted spatula. The object of stir-frying is to cook the food while moving it constantly so that it never cooks overly long on any one surface.

DEEP-FRYING

The wok is ideal for deep-frying. You may, of course, use a deep-fryer, and even a saucepan will serve the purpose. For satisfactory deep-frying, the oil should be at least 3 inches deep (and for large quantities of food, it should be deeper). A frying pan is too shallow for deep-frying.

6

The temperature of the oil is extremely important. It should not be under 325° (the food takes too long to cook and absorbs too much oil) or over 350° (the food browns without cooking through). You may wish to use a thermometer at first, but as you gain experience, you will recognize the appearance of the oil when it reaches the correct temperature. Chinese cooks stand a bamboo chopstick in the oil to test the temperature. Bubbles form on the surface of the oil around the chopstick, and if they form too quickly, the oil is too hot; if they form too slowly, the oil is too cold. Before using the chopstick to test the oil again, the chopstick should be wiped dry with a paper towel because if it becomes saturated, bubbles will not form regardless of oil temperature. As an additional test, you can drop a 2-inch bread cube into the oil. It should become a golden brown. If it cooks to a dark brown very quickly, once again the oil is too hot. If you are using an electric stove, remove the oil from the burner to cool for a few minutes, then test again. (On a gas stove you will, of course, turn off the heat.)

The same oil may be used seven to eight times for deep-frying if it isn't allowed to overheat and is cared for properly after use. Pour the oil from the wok into a saucepan to cool. If it has been used to deep-fry food coated with a dry mixture, the oil will be cloudy, but it will clear again if given a sufficient length of time to settle. The oil may then be poured off, leaving the sediment in the saucepan. Strain into a container and store at room temperature.

When deep-frying cashews, almonds, or peanuts, it is advisable to place them in a Chinese strainer so that they may be removed from the oil quickly when they reach the desired golden-brown color.

STEAMING

Steaming is a simple way to cook. It is preferable to boiling because there is no loss of natural juices and flavor to the cooking water, and the nutritive value of the food is preserved. The steam combines with the natural juices of fish or meat to make a delicious pan gravy, and steam-cooked vegetables are delicious. Steaming is an excellent way to reheat leftovers because they will stay moist, and since food can be steamed in the serving dish, it saves on dishwashing as well. If you have a bamboo or aluminum steamer, you will be able to steam more than one layer of food at a time, thus saving energy as an added bonus.

By purchasing an inexpensive steam plate, your wok may be used as a steamer. Add water to the wok to ½ inch below the steam plate. (Be sure there is enough water to last through the cooking process.) Place the steam plate in position and bring the water to a full boil over high heat. Put the dish containing the food on the steam plate, cover, and start timing the cooking.

For most steam-cooked recipes, the food is placed in a shallow dish or pie plate. This is especially important with foods such as fish or chicken, which will exude juices during cooking, and which are usually cooked in a seasoning mixture containing liquid ingredients such as soy sauce, white wine, and oyster sauce. Even foods such as dim sum must be steamed on a dish if you use a wok with a steam plate.

If you do a lot of steaming, or if you plan to make a lot of dim sum dishes, a bamboo or aluminum steamer is a worthwhile investment. The bamboo steamer is used in the wok, and its diameter must be at least an inch or two less than the top diameter of the wok. Since you will often use two layers and must have a lid to fit, it is wise to buy all three pieces at once. An advantage of the bamboo steamer is that you can cook dim sum or vegetables directly on the oiled steaming basket, and then serve them directly from the basket.

The aluminum steamer is similar to an oversized double boiler, with two layers and its own lid. This, of course, leaves the wok free for other uses. Here too, dim sum and vegetables may be placed directly on the oiled steamer. When using an aluminum or bamboo steamer, the water level for steaming should be 1½ inches below the steaming basket.

PAN-FRYING

The technique of pan-frying in a wok is simple: heat the wok, add a tablespoon or two of oil, and proceed as if using a frying pan. The Chinese cook steaks, chops, chicken, and fish this way. Using the wok for pan-frying has many advantages. An egg fried in the wok turns out perfectly round. When frying bacon or hamburger, the concave shape keeps greasy splatter to a minimum.

STEWING

To stew in a wok, cook food covered over medium-low heat. The shape of the wok causes the steam to condense and return to the stew. You will find that there is less loss of the natural juices, so more flavor is retained. Try using the wok the next time you make a stew or spaghetti sauce.

USE OF THICKENING MIXTURES

The standard thickener in Chinese cooking is cornstarch (or tapioca starch) and cold water, mixed in the ratio of two parts water to one part starch. Stir this mixture well, immediately before adding to a dish. To thicken a stir-fry dish, move the ingredients to the side of the wok. *Slowly* add the starch mixture to the liquid remaining at the center of the wok. This allows the starch to cook, and at the same time you will be able to judge how much of the mixture to use to achieve the desired texture. If you should overthicken, simply thin with a little hot water.

USE OF MARINADES AND SEASONINGS

In this book, some recipes call for a marinade, some for seasoning. The difference between the two is that a marinade is left on the meat or fish for some period of time to allow flavors to be absorbed, while seasoning is simply added to the food. Cornstarch is often used in marinades and seasoning to help the flavors adhere to the surface of the food. Marinades and seasoning can be mixed together, then added to the food; when cornstarch is one of the ingredients, however, it is easier to sprinkle the ingredients over the food and then mix well. When recipes call for a 1- or 2-hour marination, it is equally acceptable to marinate overnight in the refrigerator, if that is more convenient.

USING A MICROWAVE OVEN TO REHEAT

Most leftovers may be reheated in a microwave oven. Cover food with plastic wrap or a paper towel to prevent drying, and heat from 30 seconds to 1½ minutes, depending on quantity.

CUTTING TECHNIQUES

HOW TO SLICE FLANK STEAK

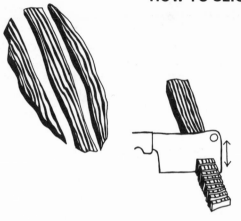

1. Trim off as much external fat as possible. Cut length-wise (with grain of meat) into 3 equal strips approximately 1½ inches wide.

2. Cut each strip crosswise (against grain) into thin slices.

HOW TO CUT FLANK STEAK INTO CUBES

1. Follow step 1, above.

2. Cut each strip crosswise (against grain) into very thin slices (approximately ⅛ inch thick), holding the cleaver slantwise at an angle of 45 degrees to the chopping board. The slices should be about 1½-by-1 inch.

HOW TO SHELL AND DEVEIN PRAWNS

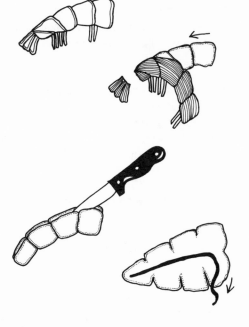

1. Starting at head, peel off shell. Remove tail.

2. Cut along back of prawn with scissors or cleaver. Run cold water over prawn and remove vein with your fingers. (The "back" is the outside curve of the prawn, and this vein often contains grit. Sometimes a vein can be seen on the "inside" curve, but this need not be removed.)

HOW TO CLEAN SQUID

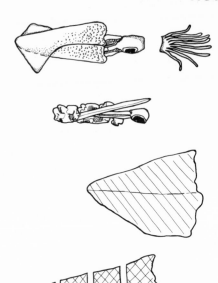

1. Cut off head and eyes and discard. Save the tentacles. (That's the best part.)

2. Slit body lengthwise and remove entrails. Using your fingers, peel off outside skin. Wash, drain, and pat squid dry with paper towels.

3. Lay squid flat on cutting board, skin side down. Score inside ¼ inch apart (do not cut through flesh), then score again every ¼ inch at right angles to first scoring. (Scoring the inside of the squid will make it curl up during cooking.)

4. Cut squid crosswise into 1½-inch pieces.

5. Leave tentacles in one piece.

12

HOW TO PREPARE WHOLE FRESH CRAB

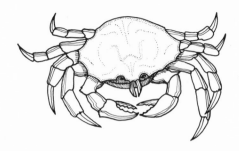

1. Insert a chopstick into the front crevice of crab, between shell and body. Use chopsticks as a lever and pull on shell at the same time, to remove shell from body. (If you buy a live crab in a Chinese market, the clerk will kill it and remove shell for you.)

2. Remove gills (fingerlike projections, or soft air sacs) by simply pulling them off. Discard. Wash crab under running water. Drain well.

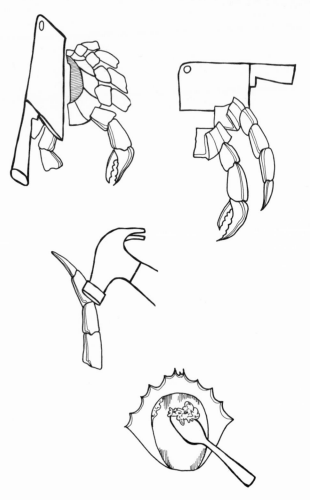

3. Using a cleaver, cut crab body up middle (through cavity left by removal of gills). Cut each half into pieces so each piece has a leg attached.

4. Crack legs with a hammer, for easier eating.

5. Scrape the yellow "crab butter" from along edges where it is attached to shell. Save this for stir-frying. Discard shell.

HOW TO CUT UP A CHICKEN

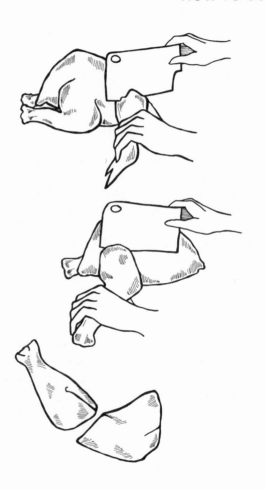

1. Place chicken breast side down on chopping block. Grasp a wing firmly. With edge of cleaver, feel for joint where it joins body. Cut through joint. Repeat with other wing.

2. Stretch leg slightly and find joint where it joins body. Cut joint. Repeat with other leg.

3. Separate thigh from drumstick by cutting through joint.

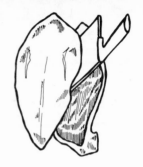

4. Grasp carcass by its back with your left hand and stand it firmly on its neck edge. Separate back from breast by cutting through rib cage. (These bones are small and cut easily. Save back for soup stock; there is little usable meat.)

HOW TO BONE CHICKEN

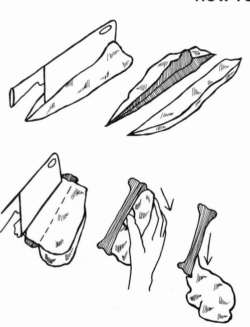

1. Remove breast skin. Place breast flesh side up on chopping block. Cut along right side of breast bone, as close to bone as possible. Turn chicken breast and repeat on other side. You should now be able to pull breast meat from each side, all in one piece. If not, cut, keeping edge of cleaver against bone, until you can free meat.

2. Remove skin from thighs. On the inside of each thigh, make a cut on each side along bone. Pull meat from bone with your fingers. Cut meat free where it is attached to bone.

3. Pull drumstick skin inside out over bottom end of drumstick. Make a cut all around lower end of bone. (Warning: there is a sharp, needlelike bone attached to main bone at upper end. Locate this and avoid it while freeing meat from bone with your fingers.) Cut meat free where it is attached to bone.

4. The "drumette" (upper, meaty portion of wing) makes an elegant hors d'oeuvre prepared this way: leave skin on. Cut all the way around lower end of bone. Push meat to top of bone (the bone acts as a convenient "handle" when served). Use drumette and lower part of wing "as is" for Deep-fried Chicken Wings.

HOW TO SLICE CHICKEN

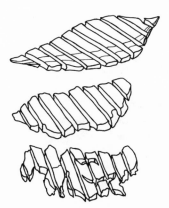

1. Slice chicken breast crosswise into ½-inch strips. Resulting pieces will be approximately 1½-by-½ inch.

2. Cut thigh meat crosswise into ½-inch strips. (These pieces will be about 1½-by-½-inch.)

3. Meat from drumsticks will have holes and will not be regular in shape. Try to cut so pieces will be about 1½-by-½ inch.

17

HOW TO CUT VEGETABLES

ASPARAGUS

1. Cut or break off tough base end of each stalk and discard.

2. With tip end of spear to your right, cut diagonally every ½ inch from right to left. Pieces should have an overall length of 1½ inches, with thickest part no more than ½ inch.

BELL PEPPER

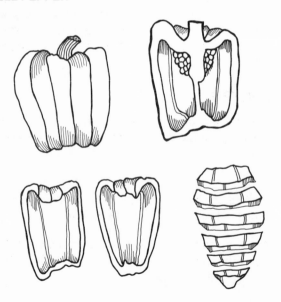

1. Cut bell pepper in half. Remove and discard seeds and stem.

2. With cut side up, cut each half lengthwise into sections 1¼ inches wide.

3. Cut each section crosswise into ⅓-inch pieces. Finished pieces will be 1¼-by-⅓ inch.

BOK CHOY (CHINESE GREENS)

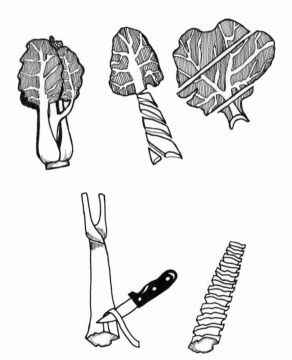

1. Break branches away from center stalk. Remove and discard any flowers and the end of the stalk.

2. Cut branches diagonally into slices approximately 1 inch long. Cut leaves in 2-inch lengths.

3. Peel off tough outside of center stalk by inserting a small knife blade under skin, holding flat of blade against your thumb, and pulling skin away (like a zipper).

4. Cut center stalk diagonally into slices ⅓ inch thick and approximately 1½ inches long.

BROCCOLI

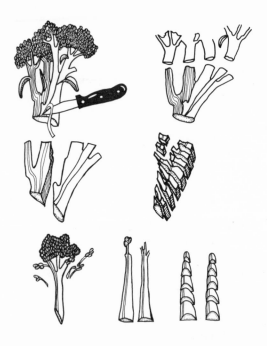

1. Peel off tough outside of stalks by inserting a small knife blade under skin, holding flat of blade against your thumb, and pulling the skin away (like a zipper). It is only necessary to peel bottom 3½ inches—top part is tender.

2. Cut stalk in half crosswise.

3. Cut bottom part of stalk in half lengthwise, and cut each piece diagonally into slices ⅓ inch thick and about 1½ inches long.

4. Break flowerettes off top of stalk.

5. Repeat step 3 with top of stalk.

CABBAGE

1. Cut cabbage in half lengthwise.

20   *(continued)*

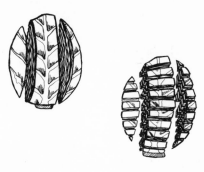

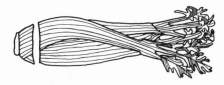

2. Place cut side down and cut each half lengthwise into sections 1½ inches wide.

3. Cut each section crosswise into ¼-inch slices. Discard core.

CELERY

1. Using a vegetable peeler, peel away stringy fibers on back of celery stalk. (Celery heart is young and tender and does not need peeling.) Cut off root end.

2. Cut celery crosswise into 1½-inch pieces.

3. Cut each piece lengthwise into strips, julienne style.

GREEN ONION

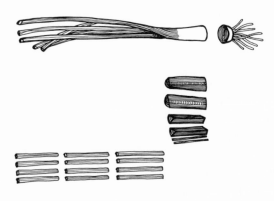

To sliver:
1. Cut off root end of onion. Cut onion into 1½-inch lengths.

2. Cut bottom pieces (white part only) in half lengthwise. Cut each half lengthwise again into 2 pieces. You may need to separate pieces by hand or with a cleaver. Leave tops (green part) in 1½-inch lengths.

To chop:
1. Follow instructions 1 and 2 above.

2. Gather slivers into a bundle and cut crosswise into ⅛-inch pieces.

1. Cut Napa cabbage in half lengthwise.

2. Place cut side down and cut each half lengthwise into sections 1 inch wide.

3. Cut each section crosswise into 1-inch pieces.

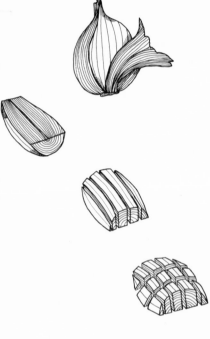

1. Peel onion. Cut onion in half lengthwise. Trim off ends.

2. Place cut side down and cut each half lengthwise into ¼-inch slices.

3. If recipe calls for diced yellow onion, cut slices crosswise into ¼-inch cubes.

USING THE FOOD PROCESSOR

The food processor is very handy for mixing and chopping fillings for pot stickers, won ton, and other dim sum items. It may be used to chop fine, or mince, any time these directions are given in the recipe methods in this book. (However, the cleaver must be used for diagonally cutting vegetables.) It is also useful for mixing dough.

MENU PLANNING

In planning a menu, the Chinese cook will select a dish from each of several categories: soup, fish, meat, and vegetable. The number of dishes selected for a meal will depend upon the number of persons to be served. Most of my recipes serve four to six persons. This is assuming, of course, that the appropriate number of dishes are served: three dishes for four people, four dishes for five people. For each additional two persons, another dish should be added.

For larger groups, it is perfectly all right to serve two or more dishes from one food category. For instance, two types of chicken may be served at the same meal. Crispy chicken, which is deep-fried, and a stir-fried vegetable with chicken would complement each other very nicely.

Rice is always served, either plain steamed rice or the more elegant fried rice. If other carbohydrates are on the menu—such as noodles, steamed buns, or flour pancakes—then it would make sense to reduce the amount of rice to be served.

In Chinese households, dim sum dishes usually are served for breakfast or lunch. However, individual dim sum items make delightful hors d'oeuvres or appetizers to serve at the cocktail hour, or as part of a dinner.

On the following page are a few suggested menus for a Chinese dinner. Each group of dishes will serve four to six persons. Add another dish for every additional two persons.

MENU 1
Dried Scallop Soup
Spring Rolls
Mongolian Chicken
Beef with Asparagus *or*
    Beef with Bok Choy
Steamed Rice

MENU 3
West Lake Minced Beef Soup
Pan-fried Pot Stickers
Clams in Black Bean Sauce
Prawns a la Szechuan
Broccoli in Oyster Sauce
Steamed Rice

MENU 5
Sweet Corn Soup
Parchment Beef
Prawns with Snow Peas
Lemon Chicken
Vegetable de Luxe
Steamed Rice

MENU 7
Fuzzy Melon Soup
Chicken with Green Beans *or*
    Chicken with Chili Peppers
Minced Squab with Lettuce Leaves
Prawns with Lobster Sauce
Steamed Rice

MENU 2
Spicy Deep-fried Beef
Mo Shu Pork with Mandarin Pancakes
Steamed Rock Cod
Bean Sprouts with Snow Peas
Szechuan-style Green Beans
Steamed Rice

MENU 4
Whole Fresh Crab in Black Bean Sauce *or*
    Whole Fresh Crab with Egg Sauce
Black and Straw Mushrooms in Oyster Sauce
Steak Cubes Chinese Style
Steamed Rice

MENU 6
Stuffed Bell Pepper
Chinese Barbecued Pork *or*
    Chinese Barbecued Spareribs
Braised Fish in Hot Bean Sauce
Szechuan-style Green Beans
Steamed Rice

MENU 8
Siu Mai Dumplings
Kung Pao Prawns
Broccoli with Barbecued Pork
Beef under Snow
Braised Fish in Black Bean Sauce
Steamed Rice

RECIPES

DIM SUM

BAKED BARBECUED PORK BUNS
焗叉燒包

Makes 15

DOUGH

1 tsp.	active dry yeast
⅓ cup	very warm (110°F.) water
2 cups	all-purpose flour
¼ cup	granulated sugar
2 tbsp.	butter, softened
2	medium eggs
½ tsp.	vanilla extract

FILLING

1½ tbsp.	oil, for stir-frying
½ cup	finely chopped yellow onion
½ lb.	Chinese Barbecued Pork, page 110, coarsely chopped
1¼ tbsp.	hoisin sauce
1 tsp.	thin soy sauce
1 tbsp.	oyster sauce
1 tbsp.	sugar
2 tsp.	sesame oil

THICKENING MIXTURE

2 tbsp.	cornstarch, mixed with
4 tbsp.	cold water

GLAZE

1	egg, beaten
Fifteen	2-inch squares of unwaxed white paper (such as typing paper)

1. To make dough, dissolve yeast in ⅓ cup very warm water. Set aside.

2. Sift flour into a large mixing bowl. Make a hole in center of flour. Add sugar, softened butter, eggs, and vanilla extract. Then slowly stir in yeast mixture.

3. Knead dough until smooth, adding a few drops of warm water if necessary. Cover with a damp cloth and set aside in a warm place to rise, for 5 to 6 hours.

4. Heat wok. Add oil, yellow onion, and barbecued pork. Stir-fry for 2 minutes over high heat.

5. Add hoisin sauce, thin soy sauce, oyster sauce, sugar, and sesame oil. Mix well. Immediately add thickening mixture. Cook for 30 seconds. Remove to a platter and let cool before using.

(continued)

6. When dough has risen sufficiently, knead lightly on floured board. Shape into a cylinder 2 inches in diameter. Cut into 15 rounds.

7. Roll each round into a ball. Flatten a ball into a 3-inch circle. Place approximately 1 tbsp. filling in center. Fold dough over filling and pinch tightly. Place sealed edge down on 2-inch square of paper. Place on a baking sheet. Repeat with remaining dough to make 15 buns. Let rise in a warm place for 1 hour.

8. Bake at 350° until golden brown (about 20 minutes). Brush with egg glaze and bake for 2 minutes more.

Advance preparation: The filling (steps 4 and 5) may be done a few days ahead and refrigerated.

Serving suggestion: May be served for breakfast, lunch, or dinner.

Note: Baked Barbecued Pork Buns may be refrigerated for up to 1 week, or frozen for up to 3 months. Reheat refrigerated buns for 10 minutes in a 300° oven. Reheat frozen buns without thawing for 15 minutes at 300°.

STEAMED BARBECUED PORK BUNS
蒸叉燒包
Makes 16

DOUGH

1 pkg.	(2 tsp.) active dry yeast
¾ cup	very warm (110° F.) water
2 cups	all-purpose flour
3 tbsp.	sugar
3 tbsp.	shortening

FILLING

1 tbsp.	oil for stir-frying
12 oz.	Chinese Barbecued Pork, page 110, coarsely chopped
¼ cup	chicken stock
2 tsp.	sugar
2 tsp.	oyster sauce
1 tbsp.	hoisin sauce

THICKENING MIXTURE

1½ tbsp.	cornstarch, mixed with
3 tbsp.	cold water
Sixteen	2-inch squares unwaxed white paper (such as typing paper)

1. To make dough, dissolve dry yeast in very warm water. Mix well.

2. Sift flour and sugar together into a large mixing bowl.

3. Add shortening and yeast mixture. Knead until smooth. Add a few drops of water, if necessary, to make a soft dough. Cover with a damp cloth and set aside in a warm place for 6 hours or more.

4. Heat wok. Add oil and barbecued pork. Stir-fry for 2 minutes over high heat.

5. Add chicken stock, sugar, oyster sauce, and hoisin sauce. Bring to a fast boil.

6. Add thickening mixture and cook for 30 seconds. Remove from heat and allow to cool to room temperature.

7. When dough has risen sufficiently, knead lightly on a floured board. Roll into a 1½-inch cylinder. Cut into 16 equal pieces.

8. Shape a piece into a 3-inch circle.

9. Place 1 tbsp. filling in center of a circle. Fold edges over filling and pinch tightly. Place sealed edge down on a 2-inch square of paper. Repeat to make 16 buns. Cover and let stand in a warm place for 30 minutes.

10. Place buns in a steamer or on a steam plate (see "Steaming," p. 7) and steam for 25 minutes.

Advance preparation: The filling (steps 4 through 6) may be prepared a few days ahead and refrigerated.

Note: Steamed Barbecued Pork Buns may be kept in the refrigerator for 1 week, or may be frozen for up to 3 months. To serve, steam for 10 minutes. (Steam frozen buns without thawing.)

CUSTARD TARTS
蛋撻

FILLING

1½ cups	water
½ cup	sugar
3	large eggs
½ tsp.	vanilla extract

PASTRY

1¾ cups	all-purpose flour
4 oz.	butter
1¼ tbsp.	sugar
1	large egg
20	tart molds, 2¾ inches in diameter

1. To make filling, bring water to a boil. Dissolve sugar in boiling water. Cool to room temperature.

2. Beat eggs and vanilla extract together. Gradually stir into the water. Mix well. Strain to remove any lumps.

3. To make pastry, sift flour into a bowl. Set aside.

4. Cream butter and sugar. Add egg. Gradually add flour (step 3), stirring in without kneading. Press together with your hands to make a smooth pastry. If necessary, add a few drops of cold water.

5. Roll out on a floured board to a thickness of less than ¼ inch.

6. Oil tart molds and dust lightly with flour. (Shake out excess flour.)

7. Cut rounds of pastry to fit tart molds. Press down into molds.

8. Add filling to ¼ inch below rim of shell.

9. Bake at 400° for about 18 minutes. Turn off oven and let tarts sit in hot oven for 10 minutes to let filling finish cooking. Insert a knife tip into center of a custard. If knife comes out clean, filling is done.

Advance preparation: Tart shells may be prepared a day ahead (steps 3 through 7), covered with plastic wrap, and refrigerated. Baked tarts may be refrigerated for a few days. Reheat in a 300° oven for 10 minutes before serving.

POT STICKERS
鍋貼料

SEASONING

SEALING MIXTURE

4 oz.	cabbage (approx. 1 cup)	¾ tsp.	salt	1 tbsp.	all-purpose flour, mixed with
1 lb.	lean ground pork**	¾ tsp.	sugar	2 tbsp.	cold water
2	green onions, finely chopped	2 tsp.	thin soy sauce		
2 tsp.	finely chopped ginger	1 tbsp.	oyster sauce		
2 tbsp.	Tientsin preserved vegetables,* rinsed and chopped	1½ tbsp.	white wine		
		2 tbsp.	cornstarch		
1	large egg, beaten with fork	1 pkg.	pot sticker skins** (about 40)		

1. Chop cabbage fine.

2. Place ground pork, chopped green onion, chopped ginger, and preserved vegetables on a chopping board. Mix and chop with a cleaver for about 30 strokes. (A food processor may be used for this step.)

3. Sprinkle on seasoning, beaten egg, and chopped cabbage to pork mixture. Mix thoroughly.

HOW TO WRAP A POT STICKER
製鍋貼方法

4. Spoon ¾ tbsp. filling in center of a pot sticker skin. Brush edges lightly with sealing mixture.

(continued)

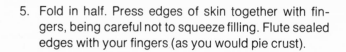

5. Fold in half. Press edges of skin together with fingers, being careful not to squeeze filling. Flute sealed edges with your fingers (as you would pie crust).

6. Grasp pot sticker along its side and gently press base on a flat surface, flattening the pot sticker so it will stand on its bottom. (The flatter they are, the less chicken stock you will need when you cook them.) Repeat to make 40 pot stickers.

Advance preparation: Pot stickers may be filled a few hours in advance and kept in the refrigerator, or they may be frozen up to 2 months, stored in a single layer in an airtight container. Thaw for no more than 30 minutes before cooking.

Note: You may choose to use half the filling recipe for pot stickers and the remainder for Deep-fried Siu Mai.

*Cabbage preserved with garlic and salt. See Glossary, page 192.

**See Glossary.

PAN-FRIED POT STICKERS
煎鍋貼
Makes 40

1	recipe Pot Stickers, page 33
2 tbsp.	oil
2¾ cups	chicken stock

DIPPING MIXTURE

3 tbsp.   thin soy sauce mixed with
1½ tbsp. Hot Oil, page 54
1½ tbsp. white vinegar

1. Heat a large frying pan (Teflon if possible, but cast iron and cast aluminum work well too. Don't use stainless

steel—the pot stickers are apt to burn). Add 1 tbsp. oil and rotate pan to spread oil evenly. Add pot stickers base side down. (An 11-inch pan will hold about 18, a 14-inch pan will hold 22.) Pan-fry base only over medium-high heat until golden brown (approximately 1 minute).

2. Add chicken stock to cover all but the top ¼ inch of the pot stickers. (In an 11-inch pan, you will need approximately 1⅓ cups, and in a 14-inch pan approximately 1⅔ cups.) Cover and cook over high heat for about 7 minutes, until all of the chicken stock has been absorbed. (Use *high* heat, even with a Teflon pan.) Then brown again until bases are crisp. (Watch carefully so they don't burn.) Remove to a platter and serve immediately with dipping mixture.

3. Repeat procedure with remaining pot stickers.

Serving suggestion: Pot stickers make excellent hors d'oeuvres.

Note: Kuo Teh is the Chinese name for the popular pot sticker. (There is some debate as to whether the name refers to the dumpling sticking to the pot in which it is cooked, or to the one into which it is ingested!) The general interpretation is that the name derives from the pot stickers being pan-fried until the bottoms are a nice golden brown. In spite of the name, they are *not* supposed to stick.

BOILED POT STICKERS IN HOT SAUCE
辣油鍋貼
Makes 40

3 qt.	water	2 tbsp.	Hot Oil, page 54
1	recipe Pot Stickers, page 33	2 tbsp.	thin soy sauce
2	green onions, finely chopped	5 tbsp.	oyster sauce

1. Bring 3 qt. water to a boil in a wok or large pot. Add pot stickers. Cook uncovered over high heat for 7 minutes.

2. Using a Chinese strainer, remove pot stickers to a large serving bowl. Add chopped green onion, Hot Oil, thin soy sauce, and oyster sauce. Mix well and serve.

Serving suggestion: Serve for lunch or with other dishes for dinner.

DEEP-FRIED SIU MAI
炸燒賣

Makes 40

1 pkg.   pot sticker skins (approx. 40)
1   recipe pot sticker filling (page 33)
1 qt.   oil

1. Prepare filling and shape pot sticker skins into siu mai (see page 37), using 1 tbsp. filling per skin.

2. Place oil in wok and heat to 325°. Drop about 15 siu mai into hot oil. Deep-fry for 6 minutes. Remove and drain off excess oil. Repeat procedure with remaining siu mai.

Advance preparation: Siu mai dumplings may be filled a few hours in advance and kept in the refrigerator, or frozen up to 2 months. Store in a single layer in an airtight container. Thaw for no more than 30 minutes before deep-frying.

Serving suggestion: Serve with Hot Mustard (page 53) as an appetizer or party snack, or as part of a dinner.

Note: Because of their shape, these are called siu mai, although they are made with pot sticker skins, not siu mai skins. You may choose to use half the Pot Sticker filling for siu mai and make pot stickers with the rest.

SIU MAI DUMPLINGS
蒸燒賣

Makes 85

18   small Chinese mushrooms (dried)
1 cup   water
1½ lb. lean ground pork*
2   green onions, finely chopped
1   egg, beaten with a fork
1 pkg. round dumpling skins*

SEASONING

1 tsp.   salt
1½ tsp.   sugar
1 tbsp.   sesame oil
4 tsp.   thin soy sauce
1¼ tbsp. oyster sauce
2 tbsp.   cornstarch

1. Boil mushrooms in 1 cup water for 10 minutes. Rinse, drain, and squeeze dry. Cut off and discard stems. Chop fine.

2. Combine ground pork, mushrooms, and green onion on a chopping board. Chop until texture resembles hamburger (about 20 strokes). Remove to a bowl.

3. Sprinkle on seasoning and egg. Mix thoroughly.

4. Use 1 tbsp. filling per skin. Place in center of a skin and gather skin up around filling (see illustration). Repeat to make 85 dumplings. Place well apart on an oiled steaming plate or steamer.

5. Steam for 25 minutes over high heat. (Repeat steaming as necessary with remaining dumplings.) Serve while hot.

Condiments: Serve with soy sauce, Hot Oil (page 54), or Hot Mustard (page 53).

Advance preparation: Dumplings may be filled a few hours in advance. Place on an oiled steaming plate or steamer. Cover until ready to steam. Dumplings may also be steamed and kept in the refrigerator for up to 1 week, or frozen for 2 to 3 months. To reheat, steam for 10 minutes. (Steam frozen dumplings without thawing.)

Serving suggestion: These make a delightful snack, or may be served as part of a lunch or dinner.

*See Glossary.

HOW TO SHAPE SIU MAI DUMPLINGS
燒賣製法

1. Spoon 1 tbsp. filling onto center of a skin.

(continued)

2. Shape dumpling into an open "basket" by pinching dough together at 4 corners.

3. Finish by pinching dough between the corners, to form 8 "pleats" in all. Leave top open. Repeat to form remaining dumplings.

PORK DUMPLINGS
粉菓

Makes 60

10	Chinese mushrooms (dried)
3 oz.	Napa cabbage, finely chopped (approx. ¾ cup)
1 lb.	lean ground pork*
1 cup	finely chopped bamboo shoots*
2	green onions, finely chopped

SEASONING

1 tsp.	salt
1½ tsp.	sugar
1 tbsp.	thin soy sauce
1 tbsp.	oyster sauce
1 tbsp.	sesame oil
Dash	pepper
1½ tbsp.	cornstarch
Sixty	2½-inch Dumpling Skins, page 42

1. Boil Chinese mushrooms for 10 minutes in water to cover; rinse, and squeeze dry. Cut off stems and discard. Chop mushrooms very fine.

2. Combine Chinese mushrooms, cabbage, ground pork, bamboo shoots, and green onions. Chop and mix with a cleaver, mincing until mixture has a fine texture.

3. Sprinkle on seasoning and mix well.

38

4. Put 1 tsp. filling in center of a skin. Fold in half and press edges together firmly with your fingers (see page 43). Repeat to make 60 dumplings. Place well apart on an oiled steaming plate or steamer.

5. Steam for 25 minutes over high heat. (Repeat steaming with remaining dumplings.) Serve hot.

Condiments: Serve with soy sauce, Hot Oil (page 54), or Hot Mustard (page 53).

Advance preparation: The dumplings may be filled about 2 hours in advance, placed in an oiled steamer or steaming plate, and kept covered until ready to steam. They may also be steamed and kept in the refrigerator for 1 week, or in the freezer for 2 to 3 months. To reheat, steam for 10 minutes. (Frozen dumplings need not be thawed before steaming.)

Serving suggestion: These may be served as a snack, or as part of a lunch or dinner.

*See Glossary.

SHRIMP DUMPLINGS
蝦 餃

Makes about 60

		SEASONING			
1¼ lb.	raw prawns in shells			1½ tbsp.	cornstarch
2 cups	water	1 tsp.	salt	Dash	pepper
2 oz.	pork fat*	1 tsp.	sugar	Sixty	2½-inch Dumpling Skins,
½ cup	finely chopped bamboo shoots**	1½ tsp.	thin soy sauce		page 42
		2 tsp.	oyster sauce		
		2 tsp.	sesame oil		

1. Shell, devein, wash, and drain prawns.

2. Bring 2 cups water to a boil. Boil pork fat for 1 minute. Drain. Chop fine.

(continued)

3. Place prawns, chopped pork fat, and bamboo shoots on a chopping board. Chop and mix with a cleaver until mixture has a fine texture.

4. Sprinkle on seasoning and mix well.

5. Put 1 tsp. filling in center of a dumpling skin. Fold in half, pressing edges together firmly with your fingers (see page 43). Repeat to make 60 dumplings. Place well apart on an oiled steaming plate or steamer.

6. Steam for 25 minutes over high heat. Repeat steaming with remaining dumplings. Serve hot.

Condiments: Serve with soy sauce, Hot Oil (page 54), or Hot Mustard (page 53).

Advance preparation: The dumplings may be filled about 2 hours in advance, placed on an oiled steamer, and kept covered until ready to steam. The dumplings may also be steamed and kept in the refrigerator for 1 week, or in the freezer for 2 to 3 months. To reheat, steam without thawing for 10 minutes.

Serving suggestion: These make a delightful snack, or may be served as part of a lunch or dinner.

*Trim from a pork butt or buy from your butcher.

**See Glossary.

HALF-MOON DUMPLINGS HOME-STYLE
蒸角子

15	small Chinese mushrooms (dried)
15	dried shrimp* (optional)
½ cup	warm water
10	water chestnuts, fresh or canned, *or*
	½ cup jicama
¼ lb.	raw prawns in shells
½ lb.	lean ground pork*
1½ tbsp.	oil
¾ cup	chicken stock
2	green onions, finely chopped
¾ lb.	Barbecued Chinese Pork, page 110, chopped fine
Forty	3½-inch Dumpling Skins, page 42

SEASONING

½ tsp.	salt
½ tsp.	sugar
1½ tsp.	thin soy sauce
½ tbsp.	oyster sauce
½ tbsp.	sesame oil
¾ tbsp.	cornstarch

THICKENING MIXTURE

1½ tbsp.	cornstarch mixed well with
3 tbsp.	cold water
1 tsp.	dark soy sauce
1 tsp.	oyster sauce

1. Soak mushrooms in warm water for 20 minutes. Rinse, drain, and squeeze dry. Remove and discard stems. Chop mushrooms fine.

2. Soak dried shrimp in ½ cup warm water for 5 minutes. Rinse and drain. Chop fine.

3. Peel fresh water chestnuts with a vegetable peeler and cut off ends (canned water chestnuts are already peeled). Chop water chestnuts fine. If using jicama, peel and chop fine.

4. Shell, devein, wash, and drain prawns. Chop fine.

5. Sprinkle seasoning on ground pork and mix well.

6. Heat wok and add oil, mushrooms, dried shrimp, and seasoned ground pork. Stir-fry for 2 minutes over high heat. Add chicken stock. Cover and cook for 2 minutes.

41

7. Add fresh prawns, barbecued pork, green onions, and water chestnuts or jicama. Toss well.

8. Stir in thickening mixture. Cook for 30 seconds. Remove mixture to a container and let cool before using. The mixture will "melt" the skin if not cooled to room temperature.

9. Put 1 tbsp. filling in the center of a skin. Fold in half. Press edges together with your fingers and pleat edges (see diagram on page 43). Repeat to make 40 dumplings. Place well apart on an oiled steaming plate or steamer.

10. Steam for 25 minutes over high heat. (Repeat steaming as necessary with remaining dumplings.) Serve hot.

Condiments: Serve with soy sauce, Hot Oil (page 54), or Hot Mustard (page 53).

Advance preparation: The filling may be made a couple of days ahead and refrigerated. The dumplings may be filled 2 hours in advance, placed in the oiled steamer, and kept covered until ready to steam. The dumplings may also be steamed and kept in the refrigerator for 1 week, or in the freezer for 2–3 months. To reheat, steam for 10 minutes. (Frozen dumplings need not be thawed first.)

Serving suggestion: These make a balanced lunch, or they can be served for dinner.

Note: You will not be able to find these dumplings in any restaurant because of the expensive ingredients. I hope you will try this recipe for yourself. It is one of my family's very favorite dishes.

*See Glossary.

DUMPLING SKINS
角仔蝦餃皮

Makes about 60

8 oz.	(½ pkg.) wheat starch*	1⅔ cups	boiling water
¼ cup	tapioca starch*	1 tbsp.	oil

1. Put the wheat starch and tapioca starch in a bowl. Mix well. Add boiling water and mix with a spoon. Cover with a damp cloth and let stand 30 minutes. (Dough will be slightly lumpy.)

2. Add 1 tbsp. oil to dough, then knead dough with hands until smooth. Divide dough into easily handled portions.

3. Shape portions of dough into cylinders about 1 inch in diameter. For pork or shrimp dumplings, cut cylinders into 1-inch pieces. For half-moon dumplings, cut into 1½-inch pieces.

4. For pork or shrimp dumplings, shape into a 2½-inch circle; for half-moon dumplings, shape into a 3½-inch circle. (A Mexican tortilla press works beautifully! If you tape a plastic food storage bag over each working surface, you won't even have to oil it.) Fill each skin immediately, otherwise it will dry out and crack when you fold it.

Note: These skins must be made at home. Unlike won ton skins and pot sticker skins, they cannot be purchased.

*See Glossary.

HOW TO SHAPE PORK, SHRIMP, AND HALF-MOON DUMPLINGS
蝦餃角仔做法

1. Spoon filling onto center of skin.

2. Fold skin in half. Press edges together firmly.

3. Pleat edges from right to left. (Pleating is not necessary, but it does make dumplings more appealing to the eye.)

(continued)

43

PARCHMENT BEEF
紙包牛肉

Makes 25

1 lb.	flank steak	
2½ tsp.	cornstarch	
2	green onions, slivered	
1½ tsp.	slivered ginger	
1 pkg.	egg roll skins* *or*	
	Twenty-five 4-inch squares aluminum foil	
1 qt.	oil for deep-frying	

SEALING MIXTURE

2 tbsp.   flour mixed well with
4 tbsp.   cold water

MARINADE MIXTURE

2 tsp.   catsup
1 tbsp.   oyster sauce
2½ tsp.   hoisin sauce
1 tsp.   thin soy sauce
1 tbsp.   white wine
Dash   pepper
1 tsp.   salt
1½ tsp.   sugar

1. Cut flank steak into 3 equal strips about 1½ inches wide, with grain of meat. Cut strips, slantwise, into ⅛-inch-thick slices (slices must be thin!). The pieces will be about 1½-by-1 inch. Put in a shallow plastic container. Sprinkle 2½ tsp. cornstarch over meat. Mix well.

2. Pour marinade mixture over the meat and mix well. Add green onions and ginger. Mix well again. Marinate at least 2 hours or overnight.

3. Separate egg roll skins. Use 1 piece of meat for each egg roll skin or each square of foil. (See wrapping instructions, next page.)

4. In wok heat oil to 325°. One by one, drop 12 packages into hot oil. Deep-fry 4 minutes on each side (total cooking time 8 minutes). Remove, using a Chinese strainer, and drain on paper towels. Repeat with remaining packages.

Condiments: Serve with catsup and Hot Mustard, page 53.

Advance preparation: Parchment beef can be wrapped 2 hours before deep-frying and kept in a covered container at room temperature. If there is more than 1 layer, separate the layers with waxed paper so they won't stick together. Parchment beef can be frozen this way for two months.

44

Defrost for 30 minutes only before deep-frying. Parchment beef may also be deep-fried several hours in advance, kept at room temperature, and reheated, uncovered, in a 325° oven for 10 minutes just before serving.

Serving suggestion: Serve as an hors d'oeuvre or with other dishes as part of a dinner.

Note: When wrapped in aluminum foil, the package must be opened and eaten from the foil. When egg roll skins are used, the entire package can be eaten, certainly a less messy procedure.

*The thinner type of egg roll skins, such as "Menlo," "Ho Tai," "Chinese Inn," or "Doll" brands, are definitely preferable for this recipe. They are a little more difficult to peel apart, but the added crispness makes the effort worthwhile. See Glossary.

HOW TO WRAP PARCHMENT BEEF
牛肉卷製法

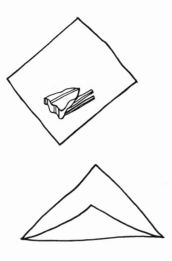

1. If using egg roll skins, peel skins apart. Put skin or foil square flat, with 1 corner toward you. Place 1 piece of beef on the skin or square, about 1¾ inches from the corner. (Be sure the piece of beef is flat.) Place 2 slivers green onion and 2 slivers ginger on beef.

2. Fold corner away from you just far enough to cover beef, 1¾ inches. (Don't fold too far—leave yourself room for 1 more fold.)

(continued)

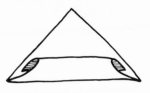

3. Fold once more, about 1¾ inches. You should now have a triangle.

4. Fold right corner, then left corner, toward center, making an "envelope" about 2½ inches wide.

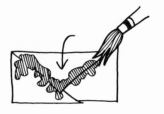

5. Brush open corner of egg roll skin with sealing mixture and fold it toward you, pressing it down firmly. Brush sealing mixture on outer edges of "flap" to help seal it. When using foil, sealing mixture is not necessary. Simply tuck in flap.

SPRING ROLLS
春卷

12	small Chinese mushrooms (dried) *or*
	1 cup fresh mushrooms
½ lb.	lean ground pork**
½ lb.	cabbage
¼ lb.	bean sprouts
1 tbsp.	oil for stir-frying
¼ cup	chicken stock
½ lb.	Chinese Barbecued Pork, page 110, finely chopped
1	green onion, finely chopped
1 tbsp.	oyster sauce
1 tsp.	thin soy sauce
½ tsp.	sugar

1 pkg.	egg roll skins*
1 qt.	oil for deep-frying

SEASONING

⅓ tsp.	salt
⅓ tsp.	sugar
½ tsp.	thin soy sauce
½ tsp.	oyster sauce
1 tsp.	white wine
1 tsp.	cornstarch

SEALING MIXTURE

2 tbsp.	flour mixed with
4 tbsp.	cold water

1. Boil dried mushrooms in water to cover for 10 minutes. Rinse, drain, and squeeze dry. Remove and discard stems. Chop mushrooms fine.

2. Sprinkle seasoning on ground pork and mix well.

3. Shred cabbage into approximately ½-inch lengths.

4. Cut bean sprouts into approximately ½-inch pieces.

5. Heat wok. Add oil, Chinese mushrooms, and seasoned ground pork. (If using fresh mushrooms, add in step 6.) Stir-fry for 2 minutes over high heat. Add chicken stock. Cover and cook for 2 minutes. Remove from heat and let cool.

6. Make sure ground pork mixture has cooled completely to room temperature. (If mixture is hot, it will break through skin.) Add barbecued pork, cabbage, bean sprouts, and green onions (and fresh mushrooms). Mix well.

(continued)

7. Add oyster sauce, thin soy sauce, and sugar. Mix thoroughly.

8. Wrap spring rolls, using 2½ tbsp. filling per roll (see page 45 for wrapping instructions).

9. In wok heat oil to 325°. Deep-fry spring rolls for 3 minutes. Turn and deep-fry opposite side for 3 minutes (total cooking time 6 minutes). If spring rolls want to roll back, hold in position with a strainer. Remove using a Chinese strainer and drain on paper towels. Serve.

Condiments: Serve with catsup and Hot Mustard, page 53.

Advance preparation: Spring rolls may be wrapped 2 hours before deep-frying and kept in a closed container at room temperature. If in more than 1 layer, separate the layers with waxed paper so they will not stick together. They may be frozen in this way for 2 months. Defrost for 30 minutes only before deep-frying. Spring rolls may also be deep-fried several hours in advance and kept at room temperature, then reheated, uncovered, in a 325° oven for 10 minutes just before serving.

Serving suggestion: Serve as an hors d'oeuvre, as an appetizer, as a snack, or combined with other dishes for dinner.

*This recipe requires the thinner egg roll skins such as Menlo, Ho Tai, Doll or Chinese Inn brands. See Glossary.

**See Glossary.

SWEET RICE ROLLS
糯米卷

1½ cups   raw sweet rice*
¼ tsp.   salt
¾ cup   cold water
2   Chinese sausages
5   small Chinese mushrooms (dried)
1 tbsp.   oil for stir-frying
¾ tbsp.   oyster sauce
½ tbsp.   thin soy sauce

1 tsp.   dark soy sauce
1   green onion, finely chopped
1 pkg.   egg roll skins**
1 qt.   oil for deep-frying

SEALING MIXTURE

2 tbsp.   flour mixed with
4 tbsp.   cold water

1. Rinse rice 4 times. Drain off excess water.

2. Place rice in a pie plate, add ¼ tsp. salt, and mix well. Add ¾ cup cold water and stir well. Place 2 Chinese sausages on top of rice. Steam for 20 minutes over high heat (see "Steaming," p. 7). Remove sausages and set aside. Mix rice so top half is turned to bottom of plate, to let rice cook evenly. Continue steaming for 15 minutes.

3. Boil Chinese mushrooms in water to cover for 10 minutes. Rinse, drain, and squeeze dry. Cut off and discard stems. Chop mushrooms into small pieces.

4. Cut Chinese sausages into small pieces.

5. Heat wok and add oil. Stir-fry mushrooms and Chinese sausages for 1 minute. Add hot cooked rice, oyster sauce, thin soy sauce, dark soy sauce, and green onion. Mix thoroughly. Set aside to cool.

6. Wrap rice rolls in egg roll skins, using 3 tbsp. filling per roll. (See page 50 for wrapping instructions.)

7. In wok heat 1 qt. oil to 325°. Deep-fry rice rolls for 3 minutes, turn, and deep-fry opposite side for 3 minutes (total cooking time 6 minutes). If rice rolls tend to roll back, hold in position with a strainer. Remove, using a Chinese strainer, and drain on paper towels. Serve.

(continued)

Advance preparation: Rice rolls may be wrapped a few hours before deep-frying and kept in a covered container at room temperature. If there is more than 1 layer, separate layers with a piece of waxed paper to prevent sticking. Rice rolls may be frozen this way for up to 2 months (defrost for 30 minutes before deep-frying). They may also be deep-fried several hours in advance and kept at room temperature, then reheated, uncovered, in a 325° oven for 10 minutes just before serving.

Serving suggestion: Sweet rice rolls make a good snack because they are quite filling. They are good for picnics also. They may be served as an hors d'oeuvre or as part of a meal.

Variations: Chinese Barbecued Pork, page 110, may be substituted for the Chinese sausage (this does not require steaming). A mixture of celery and yellow onions may be used in place of Chinese mushrooms.

*See Glossary, page 193.

**This recipe requires the thinner egg roll skins such as Menlo, Ho Tai, Doll, or Chinese Inn brands. See Glossary.

**HOW TO WRAP SPRING ROLLS
AND SWEET RICE ROLLS
春卷糯米卷製法**

1. Peel egg roll skins apart. Put skin flat, with 1 corner toward you. Spoon filling on the skin about 1½ inches from that corner.

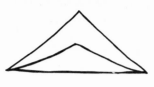

2. Fold corner away from you, just far enough to cover filling (about 1½ inches). Don't fold too far—leave yourself room for 1 more fold.

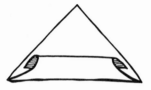

3. Fold once more, about 1½ inches.

4. Fold right corner, then left corner, toward center to form a cylinder about 5 inches long and 1½ inches in diameter.

5. Roll cylinder tightly away from you, leaving a "flap" of about 1½ inches.

(continued)

6. Brush inside edges of the flap with sealing mixture and press it down firmly. Brush outside edges with sealing mixture to complete the seal.

STUFFED BELL PEPPER
釀青椒

Makes 20 pieces

2	medium-sized green bell peppers	½ cup	chicken stock	
1 qt.	water for parboiling bell peppers	3 tbsp.	oil	
½ lb.	raw prawns in shells			
1 cup	water for parboiling pork fat			
1 oz.	pork fat* (optional)			
1 tbsp.	green onion, finely chopped			

SEASONING

½ tsp.	salt
¼ tsp.	sugar
¼ tsp.	thin soy sauce
½ tsp.	oyster sauce
1	small egg
¾ tbsp.	cornstarch

GRAVY MIXTURE

¾ tbsp.	cornstarch mixed well with
1 tbsp.	cold water
1 tsp.	dark soy sauce
1 tsp.	sesame oil

1. Cut bell peppers in half. Remove seeds. Cut into pieces about 1½ inches square.

2. Bring 1 qt. water to a boil. Add bell pepper pieces and cook for 30 seconds, uncovered (do not overcook). Remove and drain.

3. Shell, devein, wash, and drain prawns.

4. Bring 1 cup water to a boil. Add pork fat and parboil for 2 minutes. Drain and chop fine.

5. Place pork fat, prawns, and green onion on chopping board. Chop fine to a smooth texture. Put mixture into a bowl.

6. Sprinkle on seasoning and mix well.

7. Pat bell pepper pieces dry with a paper towel. Spread each piece with shrimp mixture not more than ½ inch thick, being sure to press filling down over edges of bell pepper (this helps keep filling in place while pan-frying).

8. Bring ½ cup chicken broth to a boil. Add gravy mixture to chicken stock. Cook for 30 seconds. Keep warm while pan-frying bell pepper.

9. Heat a large frying pan. Add 3 tbsp. oil. Place bell pepper pieces in pan, filling side down, and pan-fry until golden brown (about 3 minutes). Pan-fry filling side only.

10. Remove to serving platter. Pour gravy over and serve.

Advance preparation: Steps 1–7 may be done a few hours in advance and kept at room temperature.

Serving suggestion: Serve with Szechuan-style Green Beans, Mo Shu Pork with pancakes, and Steamed Rice, or use as part of a dim sum lunch.

*Trim fat from a pork butt, or buy from your butcher.

HOT MUSTARD

1 tbsp.   mustard powder   1 tbsp.   cold water

1. Mix well. Will keep in the refrigerator for a few days.

Serving suggestion: Serve as a condiment for egg rolls, Deep Fried Chicken, Barbecued Pork, or any beef dishes.

HOT OIL (Chili Oil, Hot Pepper Oil)
椒油

1 cup   oil (Safflower, peanut, or other vegetable oil   2 tbsp.   crushed dried red chili pepper
          may be used)

1. Put oil in a small saucepan. Heat for 2 minutes over medium heat.

2. Drop in a pinch of chili pepper to test oil temperature. If it turns brown, add remaining chili pepper. (If it turns black, oil is too hot. Let it cool a few minutes and test again.)

3. Remove from heat and let cool. Put in a glass container and let stand for 1 week before using. The chili pepper will settle to the bottom of the jar during this time and does not need to be removed.

Note: This oil will keep for a year or more at room temperature.

Serving suggestion: Serve as a condiment with soy sauce for Pot Stickers, Pork Dumplings, Shrimp Dumplings, Mandarin Chow Mein, and Stir-fried Rice Noodles.

SOUPS

BEAN CAKE SOUP
豆腐湯

Serves 4

½ pkg. fresh bean cake (tofu)*
¼ lb.   lean ground pork**
¼ lb.   Napa cabbage
2 sheets dried seaweed**
1 qt.   chicken stock
Salt to taste

SEASONING

¼ tsp.   salt
¼ tsp.   sugar
¾ tsp.   thin soy sauce
1 tsp.   white wine
1 tsp.   cornstarch

1. Cut bean cake into ½-inch cubes.

2. Sprinkle seasoning on ground pork and mix well.

3. Cut Napa cabbage into 1-inch pieces.

4. Rinse seaweed under warm running water. Break into 2-inch lengths.

5. Bring chicken stock to a boil. Add seaweed. Shape pork into ½-inch meatballs, and drop into soup stock. Cover and cook over high heat for 5 minutes.

6. Add Napa cabbage. Cover and cook for 2 minutes.

7. Add bean cake. Cover and cook for 1 minute. Salt to taste and serve.

Advance preparation: Steps 1 through 6 may be done a few hours in advance and stored at room temperature. Add bean cake and bring to a boil.

(continued)

55

*Buy firm bean cake (it comes in 2 or 4 pieces) for cooking. Leftover bean cake can be used for Beef with Fresh Bean Cake or Bean Cake with Ground Pork, or in any soup recipe. It needs only 1 minute cooking time. See Glossary, page 183.

**See Glossary.

BEAN THREAD AND FUZZY MELON SOUP, HOME-STYLE
粉絲節瓜湯

Serves 5

¼ lb.	lean pork butt
1 oz.	bean threads*
5	small Chinese mushrooms (dried)
1	fuzzy melon** (about 12 oz.)
1 tbsp.	oil
1 qt.	chicken stock
Salt to taste	

SEASONING

¼ tsp.	salt
¼ tsp.	sugar
½ tsp.	thin soy sauce
1 tsp.	white wine
1 tsp.	cornstarch

1. Cut pork butt into thin strips, julienne style.

2. Sprinkle seasoning on pork and mix well.

3. Soak bean threads for 20 minutes in warm water to cover. Remove and drain. Set aside.

4. Boil Chinese mushrooms in water to cover for 10 minutes. Rinse, squeeze dry, and remove and discard stems. Cut into thin strips.

5. Peel fuzzy melon. Cut diagonally into slices ¼ inch thick. Cut each slice into ¼-inch strips, julienne style.

6. Heat wok or 2½-qt. saucepan. Add oil. Stir-fry pork and mushrooms for 2 minutes over high heat.

7. Add chicken stock. Cover and bring to a boil.

8. Add bean threads. Cover and cook for 2 minutes over high heat.

9. Add fuzzy melon strips. Cover and cook for 4 minutes over high heat. Salt to taste. (Be sure bean threads are well cooked. Cook longer if necessary.) Serve.

Advance preparation: Steps 1 through 7 may be done a few hours ahead. Keep at room temperature.

Serving suggestion: This soup is served as a first course.

Variation: Napa cabbage may be substituted for fuzzy melon. Cut cabbage into strips. Use the same cooking time.

*Bean threads are also called "cellophane noodles," "long rice," or "Chinese vermicelli." See Glossary.

**Fuzzy melon is similar to a squash. See Glossary.

DRIED SCALLOP SOUP
桂花瑤柱湯

Serves 6

1 oz.	dried scallops* (3 whole)	2	eggs, beaten with a fork	**THICKENING MIXTURE**	
½ cup	warm water	Salt to taste		1 tbsp.	cornstarch mixed well with
10	small Chinese mushrooms (dried)	**SEASONING**		2 tbsp.	cold water
1	whole chicken breast (1 cup thinly sliced)	½ tsp.	salt	1 tsp.	dark soy sauce
		½ tsp.	sugar		
1	bamboo shoot** (about ½ cup, cut up)	1 tsp.	thin soy sauce		
		1 tsp.	white wine		
4 cups	chicken stock	1 tsp.	cornstarch		
		Dash	pepper		

1. Rinse and soak scallops in ½ cup warm water for 40 minutes. Shred each scallop into ¼-inch strips. Save water to add to soup stock in step 6.

2. Soak Chinese mushrooms in water to cover for 20 minutes. Rinse, drain, and squeeze dry. Cut off and discard stems. Cut mushrooms into strips, julienne style.

(continued)

57

3. Skin and bone chicken breast. Cut into thin strips, julienne style.

4. Sprinkle seasoning on chicken meat and mix well.

5. Cut bamboo shoot into 1-inch slivers.

6. Bring chicken stock and ½ cup water from step 1 to a boil. Add scallops and mushrooms. Cover and cook for 15 minutes over high heat.

7. Add chicken and bamboo shoots. Cook uncovered for 3 minutes over high heat.

8. Stir in thickening mixture. Cook for 1 minute.

9. Gradually add beaten eggs with a circular motion, then stir gently. Remove from heat immediately. Do not over-cook the egg. Salt to taste.

Advance preparation: Steps 1 through 7 may be done, and the thickening mixture prepared, a few hours ahead and kept at room temperature.

Note: This soup is expensive, but delicious! It is one of my favorite soups.

*See Glossary, page 195.

**See Glossary.

FISHERMAN'S SOUP
四色海鮮湯
Serves 6

¼ lb.	raw prawns in shells
¼ can	abalone,* optional (½ cup sliced)
10	snow peas
4	fresh or canned water chestnuts
½ can	baby corn ears ("mini-corn")**
1½ qt.	chicken stock
	Salt to taste

SEASONING

¼ tsp.	salt
¼ tsp.	sugar
1 tsp.	white wine
½ tsp.	cornstarch

1. Shell, devein, wash, and drain prawns.

2. Sprinkle seasoning on prawns and mix well.

3. Cut abalone into thin slices approximately 1 inch long.

4. Remove tips from snow peas. Cut peas in half diagonally.

5. Peel fresh water chestnuts and cut off ends. (Canned ones are already peeled.) Cut into thin slices.

6. Cut corn diagonally into ¾-inch pieces.

7. Bring chicken stock to a boil. Add prawns, water chestnuts, and baby corn. Return to a fast boil. Cook uncovered for 1 minute over high heat.

8. Add snow peas and abalone. Cook for 30 seconds, uncovered, over high heat. Salt to taste. Serve.

Advance preparation: Steps 1–7 may be done a few hours ahead and kept at room temperature.

Variation: Use bamboo shoots or chicken in place of abalone. If using chicken, slice thin and add to boiling chicken stock in step 7. Cook for 3 minutes, then add prawns, water chestnuts, and baby corn and proceed as directed.

*Be sure to buy the best-quality abalone, as the cheaper brands are tough. Leftover abalone may be stored in its own liquid, in the refrigerator, for 1 week. You may enjoy it as is, sliced, or use it in any recipe calling for abalone.

**See Glossary, page 186.

FUZZY MELON SOUP
節瓜湯

1	fuzzy melon* (about 12 oz.)	
6 oz.	lean pork butt	
1 tbsp.	oil	
1 qt.	chicken stock	
Salt to taste		

SEASONING

¼ tsp.	salt
¼ tsp.	sugar
½ tsp.	thin soy sauce
1 tsp.	white wine
1 tsp.	cornstarch
Dash	pepper

1. Peel fuzzy melon. Cut crosswise into slices approximately 1½ inches thick. Cut each slice in half lengthwise, then cut each half into ¼-inch slices.

2. Cut pork into thin slices. Sprinkle on seasoning and mix well.

3. Heat wok or saucepan. Add oil and pork. Stir-fry for 2 minutes over high heat.

4. Add chicken stock. Bring to a boil.

5. Add fuzzy melon. Cover and cook for 5 minutes over high heat.

6. Salt to taste and serve.

Advance preparation: Steps 1 through 4 may be done a few hours ahead and kept at room temperature.

Variation: You may substitute winter melon for the fuzzy melon. Use the same cooking time. You may also substitute zucchini or yellow crookneck squash, decreasing the cooking time to 3 minutes. Broccoli is also good. Cook for 3 minutes.

*See Glossary.

PORK DUMPLING SOUP
水餃湯

2 cups	water
12	small Chinese mushrooms (dried)
3 oz.	Napa cabbage for filling (about ¾ cup finely chopped)
1¼ lb.	lean ground pork*
1	green onion, finely chopped
½ cup	water chestnuts, finely chopped or ½ cup jicama, finely chopped
1	large egg lightly beaten with a fork
1 pkg.	(60) suey gow skins*
1 lb.	Napa cabbage
2½ qt.	chicken stock

SEASONING

1¼ tsp.	salt
2 tsp.	sugar
1 tbsp.	sesame oil
1¼ tbsp.	thin soy sauce
1 tbsp.	oyster sauce
2 tbsp.	cornstarch

SEALING MIXTURE

2 tbsp.	flour mixed well with
4 tbsp.	cold water

1. Bring 2 cups water to a boil. Add mushrooms and boil for 10 minutes. Rinse. Squeeze dry. Cut off and discard stems. Chop mushrooms fine.

2. Combine ground pork, chopped mushrooms, green onion, chopped Napa cabbage, and water chestnuts or jicama on a chopping board. Using a cleaver, chop and mix until well combined (about 30 strokes). A food processor may be used.

3. Sprinkle seasoning and beaten egg on pork mixture. Mix well.

4. Place 1 tbsp. filling in center of a suey gow skin. Fold in half, brush edges with sealing mixture, then press together firmly with your fingers. Place on an oiled steaming plate or steamer. Repeat until you have filled all suey gow skins. (Be sure to leave room between them so they won't stick together.)

5. Steam for 25 minutes. (Repeat steaming process until all are steamed.)

6. Cut Napa cabbage into 1-inch pieces.

(continued)

7. Bring chicken stock to a boil. Add Napa cabbage and suey gow. Cover and cook over high heat for 3 minutes.

8. Serve 6 to 8 suey gow, with Napa cabbage and broth, in individual soup bowls.

Condiment: Use individual condiment dishes containing a mixture of 1 tsp. soy sauce and 1 tsp. oyster sauce.

Advance preparation: After suey gows are steam cooked, they may be refrigerated 1 week or frozen 2 months. Cool, place in a covered plastic container, and refrigerate. Frozen dumplings need not be defrosted. Just drop into the hot soup (step 7) and cook for 3 minutes.

Serving suggestion: Serve for lunch or as a course for dinner.

Note: Suey gow soup is available in most Chinatown restaurants but is seldom found in restaurants outside of Chinatown.

*See Glossary.

SPINACH SOUP
波菜湯

Serves 4

1 bunch   spinach
½ cup   skinned and boned chicken meat
4 cups   chicken stock
½ cup   sliced fresh mushrooms
Salt to taste

SEASONING

¼ tsp.   salt
¼ tsp.   sugar
½ tsp.   thin soy sauce
1 tsp.   white wine
1 tsp.   cornstarch
Dash   pepper

1. Wash spinach thoroughly. Remove roots and cut spinach into 2-inch pieces.

2. Cut chicken into thin strips, julienne style. Sprinkle on seasoning and mix well.

62

3. Bring chicken stock to boil. Add chicken meat, stirring to separate pieces. Cover and cook for 5 minutes over high heat.

4. Add spinach and mushrooms. Cover and cook for 2 minutes. Salt to taste and serve.

Advance preparation: Steps 1 through 3 may be done in advance. When ready to complete recipe, add spinach and mushrooms and reheat to boiling.

SWEET CORN SOUP
雞粒粟米羹

Serves 5

¾ cup	skinless chicken meat (breast or thighs)	1	green onion, finely chopped	1 tsp.	cornstarch
1 tbsp.	oil	2 tbsp.	finely chopped cooked ham	Dash	pepper
4½ cups	chicken stock				

THICKENING MIXTURE

SEASONING

½ tsp.	salt
½ tsp.	sugar
1 tsp.	thin soy sauce
2 tsp.	white wine

¾ cup   skinless chicken meat (breast or thighs)
1 tbsp.   oil
4½ cups chicken stock
1   small can (8 oz.) creamed corn
½ cup   finely chopped fresh mushrooms (optional)
2   large eggs, lightly beaten with a fork
Salt to taste

1   green onion, finely chopped
2 tbsp.   finely chopped cooked ham

SEASONING
½ tsp.   salt
½ tsp.   sugar
1 tsp.   thin soy sauce
2 tsp.   white wine

1 tsp.   cornstarch
Dash   pepper

THICKENING MIXTURE
2 tbsp.   cornstarch mixed well with
3 tbsp.   cold water
1 tsp.   dark soy sauce
1½ tbsp. sesame oil

1. Mince chicken meat with a cleaver. (The texture should be like hamburger.) You may use a food processor for this step.

2. Sprinkle seasoning on chicken and mix well.

3. Heat wok. Add oil and seasoned chicken meat. Stir-fry for 1 minute over high heat, breaking meat up into small pieces while stir-frying.

(continued)

4. Add chicken stock, cover, and bring to a boil.

5. Add creamed corn, cover, and cook for 2 minutes over high heat.

6. Add fresh mushrooms and bring quickly to a fast boil.

7. Stir in thickening mixture and cook for 30 seconds.

8. Stir in beaten eggs with a circular motion. Immediately remove from heat. Salt to taste. Serve in individual bowls and garnish with green onion and ham.

Advance preparation: Steps 1 through 5 may be done a few hours ahead and kept at room temperature, or a day ahead and refrigerated.

WAR WON TON SOUP
窩雲吞湯

Serves 8-10

10	small Chinese mushrooms (dried)	2½ qt.	water
1 cup	water	1½ qt.	chicken stock
¼ lb.	raw prawns in shells	½ cup	sliced bamboo shoots
5	water chestnuts, fresh or canned, *or*	2	green onions, finely chopped (for garnish)
	¼ cup finely chopped jicama		
¾ lb.	lean ground pork*	**SEASONING**	
1	green onion, finely chopped	1¼ tsp.	salt
1 pkg.	won ton skins (contains 80)	¾ tsp.	sugar
¼ lb.	Chinese Barbecued Pork, page 110	2 tsp.	thin soy sauce
¼ lb.	bok choy	2 tsp.	oyster sauce
½ lb.	Napa cabbage	Dash	pepper
		1½ tbsp.	cornstarch
		1	large egg, lightly beaten with fork

1. Boil Chinese mushrooms in 1 cup water for 10 minutes. Rinse and squeeze dry. Cut off and discard stems. Chop mushrooms fine.

2. Shell, devein, wash, and drain prawns. Chop fine.

3. Peel fresh water chestnuts with vegetable peeler, cut off tops and bottoms and discard (canned ones are peeled and ready to use.) Chop fine. If using jicama, peel and chop fine.

4. Combine ground pork, mushrooms, prawns, green onion, and water chestnuts (or jicama) on chopping board. Mix and chop for 20 strokes. Remove to a pie plate. Sprinkle on seasoning and mix well.

5. Use 1 tsp. of filling for each won ton skin. (See directions, following, for wrapping won ton.) Do not wrap won ton more than 2 hours before using; the skins will become soggy and the filling will break through.

6. Cut barbecued pork into ¼-inch-thick slices about 1½-by-½-inch.

7. Remove outside branches of bok choy. Peel outer tough covering from center stalk and discard. Cut branches and center stalk diagonally into 2-inch pieces.

8. Cut Napa cabbage into 1-inch pieces.

9. Bring 2½ qt. water to a boil in a wok. In another wok or pot, bring 1½ qt. chicken stock to a boil. To boiling water add 40 won ton. Cook uncovered for 8 minutes. (If cooking more than 40 won ton, repeat procedure.) While won ton are cooking, add to boiling chicken stock barbecued pork, bok choy, Napa cabbage, and bamboo shoots. Cover and cook for 2 minutes.

10. Using a Chinese strainer, remove won ton from cooking water and allow to drain. Place in individual bowls. Ladle hot soup over and garnish with chopped green onion. Serve.

Condiments: Use individual condiment dishes containing a mixture of 1 tsp. thin soy sauce and 1 tsp. oyster sauce. Hot Mustard (page 53) or Hot Oil (page 54) may be used for a spicier taste.

Advance preparation: The won ton may be wrapped two hours in advance and kept at room temperature, or placed well apart on cookie sheets and frozen. When completely frozen, package. They will keep up to 3 months. Steps 6 through 8 may be done the night before and refrigerated.

Serving suggestion: This may be served as a 1-dish lunch, or with other dishes for dinner.

*See Glossary.

HOW TO WRAP WON TONS
雲吞製法

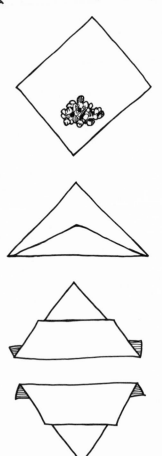

1. Place won ton skin on board with 1 corner toward you. Put 1 tsp. filling about 1 inch from that corner.

2. Fold corner away from you just far enough to cover filling (about 1 inch. Don't fold too far—leave yourself room for another fold).

3. Fold once more, about 1 inch.

4. Turn won ton so opposite corner is facing you. Dampen left corner with a little water.

5. While supporting filling from underneath with your middle finger, fold top edge of skin away from you (as tightly around filling as you can without tearing skin), placing right corner on top of dampened left corner. Press together to seal. Turn edges up for a hatlike effect.

WEST LAKE MINCED BEEF SOUP
西湖牛肉羹

Serves 5

¼ lb.	flank steak (¾ cup, minced)	2	eggs, lightly beaten with a fork	½ tsp.	thin soy sauce
5	water chestnuts, fresh or canned, chopped, *or* ¼ cup chopped jicama	Salt to taste		1 tsp.	white wine
		1½ tsp.	sesame oil	1 tsp.	cornstarch
		1	green onion, finely chopped	Dash	pepper
1 tbsp.	oil				
5 cups	chicken stock	**SEASONING**		**THICKENING MIXTURE**	
1¼ tbsp.	Chinese parsley,* minced fine (optional)	⅓ tsp.	salt	2 tbsp.	cornstarch mixed well with
		⅓ tsp.	sugar	3 tbsp.	cold water
				1½ tsp.	dark soy sauce
				1 tsp.	sugar

1. Chop flank steak with a cleaver until it is hamburger texture. (Or use a food processor.)

2. Sprinkle seasoning on flank steak. Mix well.

3. Peel fresh water chestnuts; cut off top and bottom and discard. (Or use canned water chestnuts, already peeled and trimmed.) Chop fine. If using jicama, peel and chop fine.

(continued)

4. Heat wok. Add oil and seasoned meat. Stir-fry for 1 minute over high heat, breaking up meat into small pieces while stir-frying.

5. Add chicken stock and water chestnuts. Cover and bring to a boil.

6. Add Chinese parsley and thickening mixture to soup and return to a fast boil.

7. Stir beaten eggs into soup with a circular motion. Immediately remove from heat. Salt to taste.

8. Add sesame oil. Mix well.

9. Garnish with chopped green onion. Serve.

Advance preparation: Steps 1 through 5 may be done a few hours ahead and kept at room temperature.

Note: This is a very popular soup in mainland China and Taiwan, but it is not served in many Chinese restaurants here. West Lake is a beautiful resort area in China, a favorite vacation area for several of China's emperors and their courts.

*Chinese parsley is also called "fresh coriander" or "cilantro." See Glossary, page 186.

WHITE FUNGUS SOUP
雪耳湯

½ cup	dried white fungus*
10	small Chinese mushrooms (dried)
3	dried red dates**
2 qt.	water for soaking
1 qt.	water for parboiling
½ lb.	pork butt *or*
	1 cup chicken meat
2 qt.	chicken stock
1 tbsp.	white wine
2	large eggs, lightly beaten with fork
Salt to taste	

SEASONING

½ tsp.	salt
½ tsp.	sugar
1 tsp.	thin soy sauce
1 tsp.	dark soy sauce
2 tsp.	white wine
2 tsp.	cornstarch

THICKENING MIXTURE

2 tbsp.	cornstarch mixed well with
4 tbsp.	cold water
1 tsp.	dark soy sauce

1. Soak dried fungus, Chinese mushrooms, and red dates in 2 qt. warm water for 20 minutes. Rinse and drain.

2. Cut red dates in half lengthwise. Remove and discard seeds.

3. Squeeze Chinese mushrooms to remove moisture. Remove and discard stems. Cut into ¼-inch strips, julienne style.

4. Bring 1 qt. water to a boil. Add white fungus. Boil uncovered for 3 minutes. Rinse and drain. Break up into small pieces.

5. Cut pork or chicken into thin strips, julienne style. Sprinkle on seasoning and mix well.

6. Bring chicken stock to a boil. Add 1 tbsp. white wine, mushrooms, red dates, and white fungus. Cover and cook for 25 minutes.

7. Add pork or chicken meat. Cover and cook for 7 minutes.

8. Stir in thickening mixture. Cook for 30 seconds.

(continued)

9. Gradually add beaten eggs with a circular motion. Immediately remove from heat. Salt to taste and serve.

Advance preparation: Steps 1 through 5 may be done the day before and refrigerated. Steps 6 and 7 may be prepared a few hours ahead and kept at room temperature. Reheat to boiling before completing steps 8 and 9.

Variation: If you prefer a clear soup, omit thickening mixture and eggs.

*White fungus comes in boxes weighing 4 oz. or more. Some brands are ivory in color, some light brown. See Glossary, page 188.

**See Glossary, page 193.

POULTRY

CHICKEN AND SNOW PEAS IN BLACK BEAN SAUCE
豉汁雞球蘭豆

Serves 4

1	whole chicken breast (about 12 oz. *or* 1 cup sliced chicken meat)	2½ tbsp.	oil	¾ tsp.	thin soy sauce
		¼ tsp.	salt	¾ tsp.	oyster sauce
1	green onion, finely chopped	¼ tsp.	sugar	2 tsp.	cornstarch
		½ cup	chicken stock	Dash	pepper
25	snow peas				
1 tbsp.	salted black beans*	**MARINADE**		**THICKENING MIXTURE**	
1 tsp.	finely chopped garlic	½ tsp.	salt	1 tsp.	cornstarch mixed well with
¾ tsp.	crushed dried red chili pepper**	1 tsp.	sugar	1 tbsp.	cold water
		2 tsp.	white wine	1 tsp.	dark soy sauce
		1 tsp.	sesame oil	½ tsp.	sugar

1. Skin and bone chicken breast and cut into strips about 1½-by-½-inch.

2. Sprinkle marinade ingredients on chicken and mix well. Add green onion and mix well again. Marinate for 2 hours or overnight.

3. Snap off stem ends of snow peas, then cut peas diagonally into 1-inch pieces.

4. Wash black beans twice; drain, then crush beans with butt of a cleaver. Add chopped garlic and red chili pepper.

5. Heat wok and add ½ tbsp. oil. Add snow peas and stir-fry for 30 seconds over medium heat (do not use high heat because snow peas burn easily). Sprinkle with ¼ tsp. salt and ¼ tsp. sugar. Remove from wok and set aside.

(continued)

6. Heat wok and add 2 tbsp. oil and black bean mixture. Stir-fry for 30 seconds over high heat. Add chicken and stir-fry for 2 minutes.

7. Add chicken stock and bring to a fast boil. Cover and cook for 2 minutes.

8. Add cooked snow peas, tossing lightly.

9. Stir in thickening mixture, cook for 30 seconds, and serve.

Advance preparation: Steps 1 through 7 may be done a few hours ahead. Keep at room temperature. Reheat to boiling, then complete steps 8 and 9.

Serving suggestion: Serve with Mongolian Lamb, Black and Straw Mushrooms in Oyster Sauce, and Steamed Rice.

*See Glossary, page 185.

**If you like very spicy food, increase chili pepper to 1 tsp. For a less spicy dish, it may be omitted entirely.

CHICKEN WITH CHILI PEPPERS
豆豉雞

Serves 4

1½ lbs.	chicken thighs or 2½ cups sliced chicken meat		

MARINADE

1½ lbs.	chicken thighs or
	2½ cups sliced chicken meat
1	green pepper or
	25 snow peas
3 tbsp.	oil
8	whole dried red chili peppers (optional)
⅓ cup	chicken stock
1½ tbsp.	salted black beans,* rinsed and drained
1½ tbsp.	sesame oil

1 tsp.	salt
1 tsp.	sugar
2 tsp.	thin soy sauce
2 tsp.	oyster sauce
1 tbsp.	white wine
1 tbsp.	cornstarch
Dash	pepper

1. Skin and bone chicken and cut into strips about 1½-by-1 inch.

2. Sprinkle marinade ingredients over chicken, mix well, and marinate at least 5 hours or overnight.

3. Remove and discard seeds from bell pepper. Cut bell pepper into strips 1-by-½ inch. If using snow peas, remove and discard tips. Cut diagonally into ½-inch pieces.

4. Heat wok. Add 1 tbsp. oil and bell pepper or snow peas. Stir-fry for 1 minute over medium heat. Remove from wok and set aside.

5. Heat wok. Add 2 tbsp. oil, whole chili peppers, and chicken. Stir-fry for 3 minutes over high heat.

6. Add ⅓ cup chicken stock. Cover and cook for 3 minutes over high heat. Remove and discard chili peppers.

7. Add black beans, cooked bell pepper or snow peas, and sesame oil. Mix well and serve.

Advance preparation: Steps 1 through 4 may be done a few hours in advance and kept at room temperature.

Serving suggestion: Serve with Beef with Green Beans, Salt-baked Prawns, and Steamed Rice.

*See Glossary, page 185.

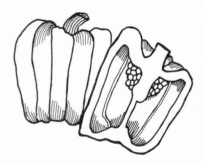

CHICKEN WITH GREEN BEANS
豆仔雞球

1 lb.	chicken thighs or chicken breasts
1 lb.	green beans
1 qt.	water for parboiling
½ tsp.	baking soda
3 tbsp.	oil
1 cup	chicken stock
1 tsp.	finely chopped garlic
1 tsp.	crushed dried red chili pepper (optional)
½ tsp.	salt
½ tsp.	sugar
1 tsp.	dark soy sauce

1 tsp.	oyster sauce
1 tbsp.	sesame oil

SEASONING

¾ tsp.	salt
¾ tsp.	sugar
1 tsp.	thin soy sauce
1 tsp.	oyster sauce
1½ tsp.	cornstarch

THICKENING MIXTURE

½ tbsp.	cornstarch mixed well with
1 tbsp.	cold water

1. Skin and bone chicken. Cut into pieces about 1½-by-½ inch.

2. Sprinkle seasoning on chicken and mix well.

3. Remove tips of green beans. Cut diagonally into 1½-inch pieces.

4. Bring 1 qt. water to a boil. Add green beans. Parboil for 7 minutes, uncovered. Add ½ tsp. baking soda to boiling water. Drain immediately. (This keeps beans a bright-green color.)

5. Heat wok. Add 1 tbsp. oil. Add chicken and stir-fry for 3 minutes over high heat. Add ½ cup chicken stock. Cover and cook for 3 minutes over high heat. Remove from wok and set aside.

6. Heat wok. Add 2 tbsp. oil, chopped garlic, chili pepper, and green beans. Stir-fry for 2 minutes over high heat. Add salt, sugar, dark soy sauce, oyster sauce, and remaining ½ cup chicken stock. Cook uncovered for 1 minute over high heat.

7. Add cooked chicken. Mix well.

8. Stir in thickening mixture. Cook for 30 seconds.

9. Add sesame oil. Mix well and serve.

Advance preparation: Steps 1 through 5 and thickening mixture may be prepared a few hours in advance and kept at room temperature.

Serving suggestion: Serve with Stewed Duck and Steamed Rice.

CURRY CHICKEN
咖喱雞球

Serves 5

1	whole chicken breast (about 1 lb. *or* 1 cup sliced chicken meat)	1¼ cup	chicken stock	1 tbsp.	oyster sauce
		1 cup	sliced fresh mushrooms	1 tbsp.	white wine
½ lb.	asparagus (1 cup sliced)			2 tsp.	cornstarch
½	yellow onion				
2 tbsp.	oil				
1 tsp.	finely chopped garlic				
1 tbsp.	curry powder				
1	green onion, finely chopped				

SEASONING

½ tsp.	salt
1 tsp.	sugar
1 tsp.	thin soy sauce

THICKENING MIXTURE

1 tbsp.	cornstarch mixed well with
2 tbsp.	cold water

1. Skin and bone chicken breast. Cut into strips about 1½-by-½ inch.

2. Sprinkle seasoning on chicken and mix well.

3. Remove tough ends of asparagus. Cut asparagus diagonally into ½-inch slices. (Each slice should be 1½ inches long.)

(continued)

4. Peel yellow onion. Cut into wedges ¼ inch thick.

5. Heat wok and add oil, garlic, and curry powder. Stir-fry for 30 seconds. Add chicken and green onion. Stir-fry for 2 minutes over high heat.

6. Add chicken stock. Cover and cook for 5 minutes over high heat.

7. Add yellow onion and asparagus. Uncover. Cook for 3 minutes.

8. Add sliced fresh mushrooms. Toss well.

9. Stir in thickening mixture. Cook for 30 seconds. Serve.

Advance preparation: Steps 1 through 6 may be done a few hours ahead and kept at room temperature.

Serving suggestion: This recipe makes a good "rice plate" served over Steamed Rice.

Variation: Broccoli, green beans, or green bell pepper may be used instead of asparagus. Green beans should be parboiled first for 5 minutes.

DEEP-FRIED CHICKEN WINGS
炸雞翼

2 lb.	chicken wings or "drumettes"
1	green onion, finely chopped
1 tsp.	finely chopped ginger
1 qt.	oil for deep-frying

COATING MIXTURE

1 tbsp.	all-purpose flour mixed well with
4 tbsp.	cornstarch
4 tbsp.	tapioca starch

MARINADE

1 tsp.	salt
1 tsp.	sugar
1 tsp.	thin soy sauce
1 tsp.	dark soy sauce
2 tsp.	oyster sauce
1 tbsp.	white wine
⅛ tsp.	five spice powder
Dash	pepper

1. "Drumettes" may be left whole or they may be boned (see page 17). If chicken wings are used, cut through joint.

2. Sprinkle chicken with marinade and mix well. Add chopped green onion and ginger. Marinate for approximately 2 hours or overnight in the refrigerator.

3. Heat oil in wok to 325°. Coat each piece of chicken with coating mixture just before dropping into hot oil. Deep-fry for 3 minutes on each side (total cooking time 6 minutes). Remove using a Chinese strainer and drain on paper towels. Serve.

Advance preparation: Chicken may be fried a few hours ahead and kept at room temperature. It may be eaten cold or reheated, uncovered, in a 275° oven for 8 minutes.

Note: Since this is a dry batter, oil will be cloudy after deep-frying. Pour off and let stand in a covered container for a day or two, then strain. The oil may be reused 7 or 8 times.

KUNG PAO CHICKEN
宮保雞

1	whole chicken breast	½ cup	chicken stock
2 cups	oil for deep-frying	1 tbsp.	hoisin sauce
½ cup	raw skinned peanuts		
3 tbsp.	oil	**SEASONING**	
1 cup	diced bamboo shoots*	½ tsp.	salt
1	green bell pepper, diced into ½-inch cubes	½ tsp.	sugar
		¾ tsp.	oyster sauce
¼ tsp.	salt	1 tbsp.	white wine
¼ tsp.	sugar	2 tsp.	cornstarch
2 tsp.	finely chopped garlic		
6	whole dried red chili peppers		

SAUCE

2½ tsp.	Japanese rice vinegar or cider vinegar, mixed well with
2 tsp.	thin soy sauce
1 tsp.	sugar
1½ tsp.	sesame oil

THICKENING MIXTURE

2 tsp.	cornstarch mixed well with
3 tsp.	cold water

1. Skin and bone chicken breast and cut into ½-inch cubes.

2. Sprinkle seasoning on chicken and mix well.

3. Heat 2 cups oil to 325° in a 1½-qt. saucepan. Put peanuts in a strainer and deep-fry until golden brown (about 3 minutes). Drain and set aside.

4. Heat wok. Add 1 tbsp. oil, bamboo shoots, and bell pepper. Stir-fry for 1 minute over high heat. Sprinkle with ¼ tsp. salt and ¼ tsp. sugar. Remove from wok and set aside.

5. Heat wok. Add 2 tbsp. oil, chopped garlic, whole chili peppers, and chicken cubes. Stir-fry for 2 minutes over high heat.

6. Add chicken stock, bring to a fast boil, cover, and cook for 3 minutes over high heat. Remove and discard chili peppers. (Leave them in if you prefer.) Add hoisin sauce and stir well.

7. Add cooked bamboo shoot mixture. Mix well.

8. Stir in thickening mixture and cook for 30 seconds.

9. Add sauce mixture and mix well.

10. Add deep-fried peanuts. Mix well and serve.

Advance preparation: Step 3 can be done up to a week ahead and stored in a closed container at room temperature. Steps 1, 2, 4, 5, and 6 may be done a few hours in advance and kept at room temperature.

Serving suggestion: Serve with Deep-fried Siu Mai, Chinese Barbecued Pork, and Steamed Rice.

Variation: Water chestnuts or jicama may be substituted for the bamboo shoots. Snow peas or zucchini may be used instead of bell pepper, using the same cooking time.

*See Glossary.

LEMON CHICKEN
檸檬雞

1	whole chicken breast (about 14 oz.) *or*
	1 cup chicken meat
½	medium-sized lemon
1 qt.	oil for deep-frying

MARINADE

½ tsp.	salt
½ tsp.	sugar
¾ tsp.	thin soy sauce
1 tsp.	oyster sauce
2 tsp.	white wine
Dash	pepper

BATTER

1	large egg white
2 tbsp.	tapioca starch*
1½ tbsp.	cornstarch

SAUCE

⅓ cup	cold water
2¼ tbsp.	ReaLemon brand lemon juice**
⅛ tsp.	salt
1 tsp.	thin soy sauce
¼ cup	sugar
1 tsp.	catsup
¾ tsp.	sesame oil
1 tsp.	cider vinegar

THICKENING MIXTURE

¾ tsp.	cornstarch mixed well with
1½ tsp.	cold water

1. Skin and bone chicken. Cut into pieces about 1½-by-½ inch.

2. Sprinkle chicken with marinade. Marinate for 1 hour if possible. (Time may be reduced if necessary.)

3. Cut lemon into thin slices, then cut each slice in half to make about 10 half slices.

4. Prepare batter by mixing thoroughly ingredients listed. (It may be necessary to add a few drops of cold water, to make a smooth batter.)

5. Prepare sauce by combining ingredients listed. Add lemon slices. Bring to a boil, stir in thickening mixture, and cook for 30 seconds. Set aside.

6. Heat oil in a wok to 325°. Add chicken pieces to batter and coat thoroughly. Drop 1 piece at a time into hot oil, stirring slightly to keep it from sticking to the bottom of the wok. Deep-fry for 5 minutes. Remove using a Chinese strainer and drain on paper towels. Place on serving platter.

7. Immediately reheat sauce to a fast boil (including lemon slices), pour over chicken, and serve.

Advance preparation: Steps 1 through 3 may be prepared the day before and refrigerated.

Serving suggestion: Serve with Shrimp Fried Rice and Beef with Asparagus.

*See Glossary.

**Fresh lemon juice is too sour. ReaLemon juice comes in plastic "squeeze" lemons and in bottles.

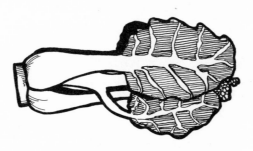

MANDARIN PRESSED DUCK
窝燒鴨

2 qt.	water
5	whole star anise*
1 slice	ginger (1 inch in diameter), crushed
2	whole green onions
1 tbsp.	salt
4–4½ lb.	fresh duck or frozen duckling
2 cups	oil for deep-frying nuts
¼ cup	raw almonds or cashew nuts
½ cup	tapioca starch** or cornstarch
1 qt.	oil for deep-frying duck
2	green onions, finely chopped

SEASONING

½ tsp.	salt
2 tsp.	oyster sauce
2 tsp.	sesame oil
1 tbsp.	white wine
Dash	pepper

BATTER

½ cup	Bisquick buttermilk baking mix
6 tbsp.	cornstarch
¾ cup	cold water

SWEET AND SOUR SAUCE

¾ cup	water
6 tbsp.	cider vinegar
3 tbsp.	catsup
⅓ tsp.	salt
¾ tsp.	thin soy sauce
6 tbsp.	sugar

THICKENING MIXTURE

1½ tbsp.	cornstarch mixed well with
3 tbsp.	cold water

1. Put 2 qt. water in a large pot and add star anise, ginger, green onions, and salt. Bring to a boil.

2. While water is heating, clean duck. Remove tail and discard; trim off fat. Add duck to boiling water. Cover and cook over medium-high heat for 30 minutes. Turn duck and cook other side for 30 minutes (total cooking time 1 hour). Remove, drain, and let cool. Discard liquid.

3. Heat 2 cups oil in a saucepan to 325°. Put almonds or cashew nuts into a strainer and deep-fry until golden brown (about 3 minutes). (Be careful! Once nuts start to brown, they overcook in a hurry.) Drain off excess oil. Chop fine. Reserve oil for step 10.

4. Remove skin from duck, keeping it as whole as possible. Spread skin flat in an 8-inch pie plate. Shred duck meat into 1½-by-½-inch strips. Place in a bowl. Add seasoning and mix well.

5. Spread seasoned duck meat over duck skin in pie plate.

6. Sprinkle ½ cup tapioca starch or cornstarch over duck meat. Press starch into meat with your hands.

7. Using a wok or steamer, steam the duck meat for 20 minutes. Let cool. Cut into 2-inch squares.

8. Combine ingredients for batter and mix well.

9. Combine ingredients for Sweet and Sour Sauce in a saucepan. Bring to a boil. Stir in thickening mixture. Cook for 30 seconds. Set aside.

10. Heat 1 qt. oil in a wok to 325°. Dip half of duck pieces, 1 piece at a time, into batter, then place in hot oil. Deep-fry for 4 minutes. Remove and drain on paper towels. Put on a platter and keep warm. Add remaining duck pieces to batter and repeat procedure.

11. Reheat Sweet and Sour Sauce to boiling (be careful not to let it boil away). Pour over duck. Sprinkle with green onions and chopped nuts. Serve.

Advance preparation: Steps 1 through 7 may be finished up to a week in advance. Steamed duck should be refrigerated (or it may be frozen for 1 month). Chopped nuts should be kept in a closed container at room temperature. Steps 8 and 9 may be done a few hours in advance and kept at room temperature.

Serving suggestion: Serve with a vegetable dish and Steamed Rice.

*A whole star anise has 5–6 points, but they are often broken. You may have to estimate the number of pieces to use to equal 5 whole ones. For more information see Glossary.

**See Glossary.

MINCED SQUAB IN LETTUCE LEAVES
白鴿粒生菜包

1 head	iceberg or romaine lettuce
1	squab* or ½ lb. pork butt
10	small Chinese mushrooms (dried) or 1 cup chopped fresh mushrooms
1 cup	warm water
2 tbsp.	oil
⅓ cup	chicken stock
½ cup	finely chopped Chinese Barbecued Pork, page 110, or cooked ham
¼ cup	finely chopped yellow onion
1 cup	finely chopped celery
½ cup	finely chopped water chestnuts (fresh or canned) or ½ cup finely chopped jicama
2	green onions, finely chopped

SEASONING

½ tsp.	salt
½ tsp.	sugar
1 tsp.	thin soy sauce
1½ tsp.	cornstarch

THICKENING MIXTURE

¼ cup	chicken stock mixed well with
1½ tsp.	dark soy sauce
1 tsp.	sugar
1½ tsp.	oyster sauce
2 tsp.	white wine
1 tbsp.	cornstarch
1 tbsp.	sesame oil

1. Carefully break off 8 outside leaves of lettuce, keeping them as large and as whole as possible. Place on a serving platter.

2. Skin and bone squab. Dice meat into ¼-inch cubes. If using pork butt, trim off excess fat and dice meat into ¼-inch cubes.

3. Sprinkle seasoning on squab or pork. Mix well.

4. Soak Chinese mushrooms for 20 minutes in 1 cup warm water. Rinse, drain, and squeeze dry. Remove and discard stems. Chop mushrooms fine.

5. Heat wok and oil. Add squab or pork meat and Chinese mushrooms. (If using fresh mushrooms, add with celery in step 6.) Stir-fry for 2 minutes over high heat. Add chicken stock. Cover and cook for 4 minutes.

6. Add barbecued pork or ham, yellow onion, celery, water chestnuts (or jicama), and green onion (and fresh mushrooms). Mix thoroughly.

7. Stir in thickening mixture. Cook for 1 minute. Remove to a serving platter. Each diner then places 2 tbsp. meat mixture onto the center of a lettuce leaf, rolls it, and eats it like a taco.

Advance preparation: Steps 1 through 5 and the thickening mixture may be prepared ahead. Heat food to a boil before proceeding with steps 6 and 7.

Serving suggestion: This may be served as a first course, or served with Black and Straw Mushrooms in Oyster Sauce, Salt-baked Prawns, and Steamed Rice.

*Since 1 squab the size of a Cornish hen now costs approximately $5, you may wish to use pork butt (about $1 worth) instead. This substitution does not change the flavor of the dish greatly, although squab is slightly sweeter. It is also rather difficult to bone a squab, due to its size.

MONGOLIAN CHICKEN
蒙古雞

Serves 4

1	whole chicken breast (about 1 lb.)	
1 tbsp.	hoisin sauce	
½ tsp.	crushed dried red pepper	
½ tsp.	catsup	
¼ cup	chicken stock	
1½ tbsp.	oil	
1½ tsp.	finely chopped garlic	
2	green onions, slivered	
1 cup	bean sprouts	
1 tbsp.	sesame oil	

MARINADE

⅓ tsp.	salt
⅓ tsp.	sugar
1 tsp.	thin soy sauce
1 tsp.	oyster sauce
2 tsp.	white wine
2 tsp.	cornstarch
Dash	pepper

1. Skin and bone chicken breast. Cut into pieces about 1-by-½ inch.

(continued)

85

2. Sprinkle marinade ingredients on chicken and mix well. Marinate for 1 hour.

3. Mix together hoisin sauce, crushed red pepper, catsup, and chicken stock in a bowl. Set aside.

4. Heat wok and add oil. Stir-fry garlic for 30 seconds. Add chicken and stir-fry for 3 minutes over high heat. Add hoisin sauce mixture and mix well. Cover and cook for 1 minute.

5. Add slivered green onion and bean sprouts. Stir-fry for 1 minute.

6. Add sesame oil. Mix well and serve.

Advance preparation: Steps 1 through 4 may be prepared a few hours in advance and kept at room temperature.

Serving suggestion: Serve with Prawns with Snow Peas, Curry Beef, and Steamed Rice.

Note: This dish does not have a gravy.

Variation: Pork may be used instead of chicken, using same cooking time.

PRINCESS CHICKEN
宮保雞丁

Serves 4

1	whole chicken breast (about 1 lb.)
⅓ tsp.	salt
⅓ tsp.	sugar
1 tsp.	oyster sauce
Dash	pepper
2 cups	oil for deep-frying
1 tbsp.	oil for stir-frying
1½ tsp.	finely chopped garlic

BATTER

1	large egg white
2 tbsp.	tapioca starch*
1½ tbsp.	cornstarch

SAUCE MIXTURE

1 tbsp.	thin soy sauce
1 tbsp.	white wine
1¼ tbsp.	cider vinegar
1 tbsp.	sesame oil
1¼ tbsp.	sugar
1 tsp.	crushed dried red chili pepper
¾ tsp.	cornstarch

1. Skin and bone chicken breast. Cut into 1½-by-½-inch pieces. Add ⅓ tsp. salt, ⅓ tsp. sugar, 1 tsp. oyster sauce, and dash pepper. Mix well.

2. Prepare sauce mixture by combining listed ingredients. Mix well and set aside.

3. Prepare batter by beating egg white lightly with a fork, then adding tapioca starch and cornstarch. Mix well. Add a few drops water if necessary. (Batter should be like thick pancake batter.) Set aside.

4. In wok heat 2 cups oil to 325°. Dip chicken into batter, drop into hot oil, and deep-fry 10 pieces at a time for 2 minutes on each side. Remove and drain on paper towels. Repeat deep-frying process until all chicken pieces are cooked. Remove oil and save. Clean wok before using again.

5. Heat wok. Add 1 tbsp. oil and garlic. Stir-fry for 30 seconds. Add sauce mixture and bring to a fast boil. Immediately add chicken, remove from heat, and serve.

Advance preparation: Steps 1 through 4 may be done a few hours ahead and kept at room temperature.

Serving suggestion: Serve with Bean Cake Soup, Clams in Black Bean Sauce, and Steamed Rice.

Variation: Fresh prawns or firm fish may be substituted for chicken, using the same cooking time.

*See Glossary.

SIZZLING RICE CHICKEN
鍋巴雞球

2 cups	hot cooked short-grain rice*
10	small Chinese mushrooms (dried)
2 stalks	celery
½ cup	thinly sliced chicken meat
2 tbsp.	oil for stir-frying
½ cup	thinly sliced bamboo shoots**
¾ lb.	bean sprouts
½ tsp.	salt
½ tsp.	sugar
1¼ cups	chicken stock
½ cup	thinly sliced Chinese Barbecued Pork, page 110
1	green onion, slivered
1 tbsp.	sesame oil
1 qt.	oil for deep-frying

SEASONING

¼ tsp.	salt
½ tsp.	sugar
1 tsp.	white wine
⅓ tsp.	thin soy sauce
⅓ tsp.	oyster sauce
1 tsp.	cornstarch
Dash	pepper

THICKENING MIXTURE

1½ tbsp.	cornstarch, mixed well with
3 tbsp.	cold water
1 tsp.	dark soy sauce
1 tsp.	oyster sauce

1. Press hot cooked rice into 3-inch squares ¼-inch thick on an oiled cookie sheet. Rice must be hot in order to stick together in a pattie. Bake at 300° for 25 minutes, turn, and bake other side for 25 minutes (total cooking time 50 minutes). Rice patties should be an ivory color. Baking is to keep rice patties together, not to brown rice. Remove and set aside.

2. Boil Chinese mushrooms in water to cover for 10 minutes. Rinse, drain, and squeeze dry. Remove and discard stems. Cut mushrooms into ¼-inch strips.

3. Peel celery. Cut into 1½-inch pieces, then cut each piece lengthwise into strips, julienne style.

4. Sprinkle seasoning on chicken and mix well.

5. Heat wok. Add 1 tbsp. oil, celery, bamboo shoots, and bean sprouts. Stir-fry for 2 minutes over high heat. Sprinkle with ½ tsp. salt and ½ tsp. sugar. Remove from wok and set aside.

6. Heat wok and add 1 tbsp. oil, mushrooms, and chicken. Stir-fry for 2 minutes over high heat. Add chicken stock, cover, and cook for 4 minutes. Add celery mixture, barbecued pork, slivered green onion, and sesame oil. Mix well. Remove from heat (leave in wok; do not cover).

7. Heat 1 qt. oil in another wok or a saucepan to 325°. Deep-fry rice patties approximately 2 minutes on each side until golden brown. After they have cooked about 3 minutes, reheat chicken mixture from step 6, add thickening mixture, and cook for 30 seconds. By this time, rice patties should be golden brown.

8. Remove rice patties immediately to a large serving platter. Pour hot chicken mixture over rice patties and serve. (If chicken mixture and rice patties are finished at the same moment and really hot, the dish will sizzle.)

Advance preparation: Steps 1 through 6 may be done ahead and kept at room temperature. Baked rice patties will keep 1 week in the refrigerator in a closed container, or 1 day at room temperature.

Serving suggestion: Serve with Kung Pao Prawns, Mongolian Lamb, and Steamed Rice.

*Short-grain (Calrose) rice is more glutinous than long-grain rice and makes a better pattie. It is cooked the same way as Steamed Rice, page 179.

**See Glossary.

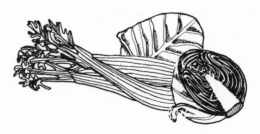

STEWED CHICKEN
焗雞

30	small Chinese mushrooms (dried)
2 cups	warm water
20	lily flowers*
4 pieces	dried black fungus** (¾ cup soaked and sliced)
1 cup	warm water
2	green onions
1	3½–4-lb. whole fresh chicken
1 tbsp.	dark soy sauce
3 tbsp.	oil
1 tsp.	salt
1 qt.	chicken stock
1 slice	ginger (1 inch diameter) ½ inch thick, crushed

SEASONING

2 tbsp.	white wine
1 tbsp.	thin soy sauce
2 tsp.	sugar
1½ tbsp.	oyster sauce
Dash	pepper

THICKENING MIXTURE

2 tbsp.	cornstarch mixed well with
4 tbsp.	cold water

1. Soak mushrooms in 2 cups warm water for 20 minutes. Rinse and squeeze dry. Remove and discard stems. Leave mushrooms whole.

2. Soak lily flowers and dried fungus in 1 cup warm water for 10 minutes. Rinse and squeeze dry. Cut off and discard ¼ inch from pointed end of lily flowers. Remove and discard stems from fungus. Cut fungus into 1-inch pieces.

3. Cut green onions in half lengthwise.

4. Wash chicken. Drain and pat dry with a paper towel. Rub skin with 1 tbsp. dark soy sauce.

5. Heat wok. Add 3 tbsp. oil. Add chicken, breast side down, and pan-fry until golden brown (about 3 minutes) over medium heat. Turn and pan-fry back until golden brown (about 3 minutes). Then pan-fry each drumstick side until golden brown (about 3 minutes). Remove to a platter and sprinkle 1 tsp. salt evenly over chicken skin. Set aside.

90

6. In clean wok, put 1 qt. chicken stock, green onion, ginger, mushrooms, and seasoning mixture. Stir well and bring to a boil.

7. Add chicken, breast side down. Cover and cook over medium-high heat for 15 minutes. Turn and cook for 15 minutes more on its back. Turn to drumstick side and cook for 10 minutes. Turn to other drumstick side. Add lily flowers and fungus and cook for 10 minutes. Remove chicken and let cool.

8. When cool, chop chicken into serving-size pieces (about 2 inches square).

9. Remove green onion and ginger from liquid and discard. There should be 1½ cups of liquid remaining. If not, add sufficient chicken stock to make 1½ cups.

10. Bring liquid, containing mushrooms, lily flowers and fungus, to a boil. Stir in part of thickening mixture and cook for 1 minute. If a thicker gravy is desired, stir in remaining thickening mixture and cook for 1 minute. Pour hot gravy over chicken and serve.

Advance preparation: Steps 1 through 3 may be done a day ahead and refrigerated. Steps 4 through 9 can be prepared a few hours ahead and kept at room temperature.

Serving suggestion: This is a main-course recipe. Serve with any vegetable dish and Steamed Rice.

*See Glossary.

**See Glossary, page 188.

STEWED DUCK
西湖鴨

1 head	iceberg lettuce *or*
	2 bunches spinach
1 slice	ginger (1 inch diameter) 1 inch thick
2	green onions
1 piece	dried tangerine peel* (2-inch strip)
1 bunch	Chinese parsley* (optional)
1	fresh whole duck (4½ lbs.)
1 tbsp.	dark soy sauce (for rubbing duck skin)
1 qt.	oil for deep-frying
1 tsp.	salt
1½ qt.	chicken stock
4 whole	star anise*
¼ tsp.	five-spice powder*

2 tsp.	finely chopped garlic
2 tbsp.	oyster sauce
1½ qt.	water

SEASONING

3 tbsp.	white wine
1 tbsp.	thin soy sauce
1 tbsp.	dark soy sauce
2 tsp.	sugar
⅛ tsp.	pepper

THICKENING MIXTURE

3½ tbsp.	cornstarch mixed well with
5 tbsp.	cold water

1. Wash lettuce or spinach. (If using spinach, trim off stem ends.) Cut into 2-inch pieces.

2. Peel and crush ginger.

3. Cut green onions in half lengthwise.

4. Rinse tangerine peel and break into 4 equal pieces.

5. Remove stem ends of Chinese parsley, rinse, and drain.

6. Wash duck, drain, and pat dry with a paper towel. Rub skin with 1 tbsp. dark soy sauce.

7. Heat 1 qt. oil in a wok to 325°. Deep-fry duck, breast side down, until golden brown (approximately 2 minutes). Turn and deep-fry back until golden brown (approximately 2 minutes). Then deep-fry each drumstick side for

2 minutes, until golden brown. (The deep-frying improves the appearance of the duck as well as the texture and flavor of the skin.) Remove to a roasting pan. Sprinkle 1 tsp. salt over duck skin. Remove oil from wok and wipe wok dry.

8. Put 1½ qt. chicken stock in wok. Add ginger, green onion, tangerine peel, star anise, five-spice powder, garlic, and seasoning mixture. Bring to a boil.

9. Add duck, breast side down. Cover and cook for 45 minutes over medium heat. Turn and cook on its back for 45 minutes more (total cooking time 1½ hours), checking level of chicken stock periodically (you may need to add more). There should be 3 cups liquid remaining when cooking is complete. Remove duck to the roasting pan and keep warm.

10. Remove as much fat as possible from remaining liquid. Strain into a saucepan (to remove tangerine peel, star anise, etc.). Add oyster sauce.

11. Bring liquid to a boil. Stir in part of thickening mixture and cook for 1 minute. If necessary, add more thickening mixture to adjust consistency of gravy and cook for 1 minute. Keep warm over low heat.

12. Bring 1½ qt. water to a boil. Add lettuce or spinach and cook uncovered for 2 minutes. Drain. Place on a large serving platter. Place duck on bed of vegetables. Pour hot gravy over duck. Garnish with Chinese parsley. Serve. Each diner then serves himself.

Advance preparation: Steps 1 through 10 may be done a few hours in advance. Put the duck back into the liquid and reheat, covered, before proceeding with the recipe.

Serving suggestion: This elegant dish requires considerable work to prepare and serves a large number. It should be the star of the show, served with steamed rice only.

*See Glossary.

SZECHUAN SPICED CHICKEN
四川辣雞

1	whole chicken breast (about 12 oz.) *or* 1 cup sliced chicken meat
1	green bell pepper *or* 25 snow peas
Dash	salt
Dash	sugar
2 tbsp.	oil
½ cup	chicken stock
2	green onions, slivered

SAUCE

1 tsp.	chili paste with garlic*
1 tsp.	hoisin sauce
1 tsp.	sugar
1½ tsp.	Japanese rice vinegar
1 tsp.	dark soy sauce
1 tsp.	oyster sauce
2 tsp.	sesame oil

SEASONING

⅓ tsp.	salt
½ tsp.	sugar
½ tsp.	thin soy sauce
1 tsp.	oyster sauce
2 tsp.	white wine
2 tsp.	cornstarch
Dash	pepper

THICKENING MIXTURE

1 tsp.	cornstarch mixed well with
2 tsp.	cold water

1. Skin and bone chicken. Cut into strips 1½-by-½ inch.

2. Sprinkle seasoning on chicken and mix well.

3. Remove seeds from bell pepper. Cut into strips 1½ by ¼ inch. If using snow peas, remove tips and cut peas diagonally into pieces about ½ inch wide.

4. Prepare sauce by combining listed ingredients. Set aside.

5. Heat wok. Add ½ tbsp. oil. Stir-fry bell pepper or snow peas for 1 minute. Sprinkle with a dash of salt and a dash of sugar. Remove from wok and set aside.

6. Heat wok. Add 1½ tbsp. oil. Stir-fry seasoned chicken for 2 minutes over high heat.

7. Add chicken stock. Bring to a fast boil, cover, and cook for 2 minutes over high heat. Add sauce and stir well.

8. Add bell pepper strips (or snow peas) and slivered green onions. Toss well.

9. Add thickening mixture. Cook for 30 seconds. Serve.

Advance preparation: Steps 1 through 7 may be done a few hours ahead. Keep at room temperature until ready to complete recipe.

Serving suggestion: Serve with Mandarin Chow Mein, Broccoli in Oyster Sauce, and Steamed Rice.

*Chili paste with garlic is quite spicy. For a milder flavor, reduce amount to ½ tsp. See Glossary.

VELVET CHICKEN
生炒雞片

Serves 4

1	whole chicken breast (about 12 oz.) *or*	**MARINADE**	
	1 cup sliced chicken meat	½ tsp.	salt
1 tsp.	finely chopped garlic	1 tsp.	sugar
1 tsp.	finely chopped ginger	2 tsp.	white wine
1	green onion, finely chopped	1 tsp.	sesame oil
25	snow peas	¾ tsp.	thin soy sauce
3 tbsp.	oil	1 tsp.	oyster sauce
¼ tsp.	salt	Dash	pepper
¼ tsp.	sugar	2 tsp.	cornstarch
½ cup	chicken stock		
2	egg whites, lightly beaten with fork		

1. Skin and bone chicken breast. Cut into strips 1½-by-½ inch.

2. Sprinkle marinade ingredients on chicken and mix well. Add chopped garlic, ginger, and green onion and mix well again. Marinate for 2 hours.

3. Snap off stem ends of snow peas. Cut peas diagonally into 1-inch pieces.

4. Heat wok. Add 1 tbsp. oil and snow peas. Stir-fry 30 seconds over medium heat. (Be careful! They burn easily.) Remove from wok and set aside.

(continued)

5. Heat wok. Add 2 tbsp. oil and chicken. Stir-fry 2 minutes over high heat. Add salt, sugar, and chicken stock. Bring to a fast boil. Cook uncovered for 2 minutes.

6. Add cooked snow peas. Toss lightly.

7. Add beaten egg whites, mix well, and serve.

Advance preparation: Steps 1 through 5 may be done ahead. Reheat to boiling and complete steps 6 and 7.

Serving suggestion: Serve with War Won Ton Soup, Asparagus in Black Bean Sauce, and Steamed Rice.

MEATS

BEEF UNDER SNOW
炒假綿羊

Serves 4

½ lb.	flank steak	½ cup	shredded bamboo shoots*	1½ tsp.	cornstarch
10	snow peas	⅓ cup	chicken stock	Dash	pepper
3 cups	oil for deep-frying				
1 oz.	rice sticks*	**MARINADE**		**THICKENING MIXTURE**	
2 tbsp.	oil for stir-frying	⅓ tsp.	salt	1 tsp.	cornstarch mixed well with
1 tsp.	chili paste with garlic*	½ tsp.	sugar	2 tsp.	cold water
10	fresh mushrooms, sliced	1 tsp.	thin soy sauce	1 tsp.	dark soy sauce
2	green onions, slivered	1½ tsp.	white wine	2 tsp.	sesame oil
		1 tsp.	oyster sauce		

1. Cut flank steak (with grain of meat) into 3 equal strips approximately 1½ inches wide. Cut each strip across the grain into thin slices.

2. Sprinkle marinade ingredients over beef and mix well. Marinate 1 hour.

3. Remove and discard tips from snow peas. Cut peas into thin strips, julienne style.

4. Heat 3 cups oil in a wok to 325°. Drop in 1 rice stick to test oil temperature. It should puff up immediately. If it doesn't, oil is not hot enough. Deep-fry ½ oz. rice sticks. Turn and deep-fry bottom side if necessary. Remove to paper towels to drain excess oil. Repeat deep-frying process with remainder of rice sticks. Break up rice sticks to approximately 2-inch lengths. Remove oil from wok.

5. Heat wok. Add 2 tbsp. oil and flank steak. Stir-fry for 3 minutes over high heat. Add chili paste with garlic; stir well.

(continued)

6. Add snow peas, fresh mushrooms, green onion, and bamboo shoots. Stir-fry for 1 minute over high heat. Add chicken stock. Bring quickly to a fast boil.

7. Stir in thickening mixture. Cook for 30 seconds. Remove to serving platter. Sprinkle rice sticks over the top. Serve immediately.

Advance preparation: Step 4 may be done several days ahead. Store in an airtight container. (Rice sticks need not be hot.) Steps 1 through 3 may be done several hours in advance and kept at room temperature, or the night before and refrigerated.

Serving suggestion: Serve with Lemon Chicken and Sweet Rice Rolls.

*See Glossary.

BEEF WITH ASPARAGUS
鼓汁牛肉梨箭

Serves 6

½ lb.	flank steak
1	green onion, slivered
1¼ lb.	fresh asparagus
1½ tbsp.	salted black beans*
1 tsp.	finely chopped garlic
1 tsp.	crushed dried red chili pepper (optional)
3 tbsp.	oil
½ tsp.	salt
½ tsp.	sugar
¾ cup	chicken stock
1 tbsp.	sesame oil

SEASONING

½ tsp.	salt
¼ tsp.	sugar
2 tsp.	white wine
½ tsp.	thin soy sauce
1½ tsp.	oyster sauce
½ tbsp.	cornstarch
Dash	pepper

THICKENING MIXTURE

¾ tbsp. cornstarch mixed well with
1½ tbsp. cold water

1. Cut flank steak (with grain of meat) into 3 equal strips about 1½ inches wide. Cut each strip across grain into thin slices.

2. Sprinkle seasoning on beef and mix well. Then add slivered green onion.

3. Break off and discard tough, base-end of asparagus. Cut each spear diagonally into slices ½ inch thick and 1½ inches long.

4. Rinse black beans twice. Drain. Mash into a paste with butt of a cleaver. Add chopped garlic and crushed red pepper. Mix well.

5. Heat wok and add 1½ tbsp. oil. Stir-fry beef for 3 minutes over high heat. Remove from wok and set aside.

6. Heat wok and 1½ tbsp. oil and black bean mixture. Stir-fry for 30 seconds over high heat.

7. Add asparagus and stir-fry for 2 minutes over high heat. Add salt, sugar, and chicken stock. Bring quickly to a fast boil and cook, uncovered, for 2 minutes.

8. Add cooked beef and mix well.

9. Stir in thickening mixture and cook for 30 seconds.

10. Add sesame oil. Mix well and serve.

Advance preparation: Steps 1 through 5 may be done a few hours in advance and kept at room temperature.

Serving suggestion: Serve with West Lake Minced Beef Soup, Eight Flavors Steamed Fish, and Steamed Rice.

Variation: Broccoli or bok choy may be substituted for the asparagus, using the same cooking time.

*See Glossary, page 185.

BEEF WITH BITTER MELON
苦瓜牛肉

2	bitter melons* (1¼ lb.)
¼ tsp.	salt (for soaking)
1½ qt.	water
½ lb.	flank steak
2 tbsp.	salted black beans**
2 tsp.	finely chopped garlic
2½ tbsp.	oil
2 tsp.	sugar
1 tbsp.	oyster sauce
1¼ cups	chicken stock

SEASONING

½ tsp.	salt
½ tsp.	sugar
2 tsp.	white wine
½ tsp.	thin soy sauce
1½ tsp.	oyster sauce
½ tbsp.	cornstarch
Dash	pepper

THICKENING MIXTURE

1¾ tsp.	cornstarch mixed well with
1 tbsp.	cold water
1 tsp.	dark soy sauce

1. Cut bitter melons in half lengthwise. Remove and discard seeds. Trim ends and discard. Cut each half cross-wise into thin slices, less than ¼ inch thick. Put into a colander and sprinkle with ¼ tsp. salt. Mix well and let stand for 2 hours. After 2 hours, squeeze melon slices gently to remove liquid (this helps remove some of the bitterness).

2. Bring 1½ qt. water to a boil. Add bitter melon. Boil, uncovered, for 5 minutes. Remove to a colander, rinse under cold water, and drain. Squeeze out excess liquid.

3. Cut flank steak lengthwise (with grain of meat) into 3 equal strips, about 1½ inches wide. Cut each strip across grain into thin slices.

4. Sprinkle seasoning on beef and mix well.

5. Rinse black beans 2 times. Drain. Mash into a paste with the butt of a cleaver. Add chopped garlic.

6. Heat wok and add 1 tbsp. oil and beef. Stir-fry over high heat for 3 minutes. Remove from wok and set aside.

7. Heat wok. Add 1½ tbsp. oil, black bean mixture, and bitter melon. Stir-fry for 3 minutes over high heat.

8. Add sugar, oyster sauce, and chicken stock. Bring to a fast boil, cover, and cook for 3 minutes.

9. Add cooked beef and toss well.

10. Stir in thickening mixture. Cook 30 seconds. Serve.

Advance preparation: Steps 1 through 8 may be completed a few hours ahead and kept at room temperature.

Serving suggestion: Serve with Fuzzy Melon Soup, Jennie's Steamed Pork Cake, and Steamed Rice.

Note: Bitter melon is definitely an acquired taste. The older generation of Chinese enjoy it, but few of the younger generation do. You may wish to try this recipe to sample authentic Chinese cuisine.

*See Glossary.

**See Glossary, page 185.

BEEF WITH BOK CHOY
牛肉炒白菜

Serves 5

¾ lb.	flank steak
1	green onion, slivered
1½ lb.	bok choy
2½ tbsp.	oil
2 tsp.	finely chopped garlic
½ tsp.	salt
½ tsp.	sugar
¾ cup	chicken stock

SEASONING

½ tsp.	salt
1 tsp.	sugar
2 tsp.	white wine
1½ tsp.	thin soy sauce
1½ tsp.	oyster sauce
1 tsp.	sesame oil
2 tsp.	cornstarch
Dash	pepper

THICKENING MIXTURE

1 tsp.	cornstarch mixed well with
2 tsp.	cold water
1 tsp.	dark soy sauce

1. Cut flank steak lengthwise (with grain of meat) into 3 equal strips about 1½ inches wide. Cut each strip across grain into thin slices.

2. Sprinkle seasoning on beef and mix well. Add slivered green onion.

3. Break branches off center stalk of bok choy, removing and discarding any flowers. Trim stem end of each leaf where it joined the center stalk. Cut stems and leaves diagonally into 2-inch pieces. Peel off and discard tough skin of center stalk. Cut stalk diagonally into 2-inch lengths.

(continued)

4. Heat wok. Add 1½ tbsp. oil and chopped garlic. Stir-fry for 30 seconds over high heat. Add flank steak and stir-fry for 2 minutes. Remove from wok and set aside.

5. Heat wok. Add 1 tbsp. oil and bok choy. Stir-fry for 2 minutes. Add salt, sugar, and chicken stock. Bring to a fast boil. Cook, uncovered, for 1 minute.

6. Add cooked flank steak and mix well. Cook for 1 minute. (Make sure all beef is cooked to your preference.)

7. Stir in thickening mixture. Cook 30 seconds longer and serve.

Advance preparation: Steps 1 through 4 may be prepared a few hours ahead and kept at room temperature until you are ready to complete dish.

Serving suggestion: Serve with Sizzling Rice Chicken, Butterfly Prawns, and Steamed Rice.

Variation: Broccoli, asparagus, zucchini, or summer squash may be substituted for the bok choy. The cooking time will be the same.

BEEF WITH GREEN BEANS
青豆牛肉

Serves 4

½ lb.	flank steak
1	green onion, slivered
1 lb.	green beans
1 qt.	water
1 tbsp.	hot bean sauce*
2 tsp.	finely chopped garlic
2½ tbsp.	oil
⅓ tsp.	salt

| ⅓ tsp. | sugar |
| ¾ cup | chicken stock |

SEASONING

⅓ tsp.	salt
¾ tsp.	sugar
1½ tsp.	white wine
1 tsp.	thin soy sauce

1 tsp.	oyster sauce
1 tsp.	sesame oil
1½ tsp.	cornstarch
Dash	pepper

THICKENING MIXTURE

| 1 tsp. | cornstarch mixed well with |
| 2 tsp. | cold water |

1. Cut flank steak lengthwise (with grain of meat) into 3 equal strips approximately 1½ inches wide. Cut each strip across grain into thin slices.

2. Sprinkle seasoning on flank steak and mix well. Add slivered green onion.

3. Remove tips from green beans. Cut beans diagonally into 1½-inch pieces.

4. Bring 1 qt. water to a boil. Add green beans. Boil, uncovered, for 7 minutes. (You may prefer beans cooked a little longer.) Drain.

5. Mash bean sauce into a paste with butt of a cleaver. Add chopped garlic.

6. Heat wok. Add 1 tbsp. oil and flank steak. Stir-fry for 2 minutes over high heat. Remove from wok and set aside.

7. Heat wok. Add 1½ tbsp. oil and green beans. Stir-fry for 1½ minutes over high heat. Add ⅓ tsp. salt, ⅓ tsp. sugar, and bean sauce; mix well. Add chicken stock. Bring to a fast boil. Cook uncovered for 1 minute.

8. Add cooked flank steak. Mix well. Cook for 30 seconds over high heat, or until beef is cooked to your liking.

9. Stir in thickening mixture, cook for 30 seconds, and serve.

Advance preparation: Steps 1 through 6 and the thickening mixture may be prepared a few hours ahead and kept at room temperature until ready to complete the dish.

Serving suggestion: Serve with Stuffed Bell Peppers, Braised Fish with Black Bean Sauce, and Steamed Rice.

*Szechuan-style bean sauce is quite spicy. Cantonese-style bean sauce may be substituted if you prefer less spicy food. See Glossary, page 184.

CURRY BEEF
咖喱牛肉   Serves 4

½ lb.	flank steak	½ tsp.	sugar	½ tbsp.	white wine
1	green onion, slivered	1¼ tbsp.	curry powder	½ tbsp.	cornstarch
2 stalks	celery	1 cup	chicken stock		
½	green bell pepper			**THICKENING MIXTURE**	
½	yellow onion	**SEASONING**		2 tsp.	cornstarch mixed well with
2	medium-sized tomatoes	½ tsp.	salt	1 tbsp.	cold water
2 tbsp.	oil	½ tsp.	sugar	1 tsp.	sugar
½ tsp.	salt	1 tsp.	thin soy sauce	1 tsp.	dark soy sauce
		1¼ tsp.	oyster sauce		

(continued)

1. Cut flank steak (with grain of meat) into 3 equal strips about 1½ inches wide. Cut each strip across grain into thin slices.

2. Sprinkle seasoning on beef and mix well. Then add slivered green onion.

3. Remove celery strings with a vegetable peeler. Cut celery into 1½-inch pieces. Cut each piece into strips, julienne style.

4. Remove seeds from bell pepper and cut pepper into pieces 1-by-½ inch.

5. Cut yellow onion into ¼-inch wedges.

6. Cut tomatoes in half, then cut each half into 4 wedges.

7. Heat wok. Add ½ tbsp. oil, celery, bell pepper, and yellow onion. Stir-fry for 2 minutes over high heat. Sprinkle with ½ tsp. salt and ½ tsp. sugar. Remove from wok and set aside.

8. Heat wok. Add 1½ tbsp. oil, curry powder, and beef. Stir-fry for 3 minutes over high heat.

9. Add chicken stock and tomatoes. Bring quickly to a fast boil.

10. Add cooked vegetables. Toss well.

11. Stir in thickening mixture. Mix well. Serve.

Advance preparation: Steps 1 through 6 may be done the day before and refrigerated or a few hours ahead and kept at room temperature.

Serving suggestion: Serve with Kung Pao Prawns, Spiced Pork, and Steamed Rice.

SPICY DEEP-FRIED BEEF
炸辣牛肉

Serves 4

½ lb.	flank steak
1 tbsp.	raw sesame seeds
3 cups	oil for deep-frying
1	large egg white, lightly beaten with fork
¾ cup	cornstarch
1 tbsp.	oil for stir-frying
1 tsp.	finely chopped garlic

MARINADE

¼ tsp.	baking soda
1 tsp.	sugar
½ tsp.	salt
1 tsp.	thin soy sauce
1 tsp.	oyster sauce
½ tbsp.	white wine
Dash	pepper

SAUCE

¼ cup	chicken stock
1½ tbsp.	thin soy sauce
1½ tbsp.	sesame oil
2 tbsp.	sugar
1½ tbsp.	white wine
2 tsp.	oyster sauce
½ tsp.	crushed dried red chili pepper

THICKENING MIXTURE

1¼ tsp.	cornstarch mixed well with
2 tsp.	cold water

1. Cut flank steak lengthwise (with grain of meat) into 3 equal strips approximately 1½ inches wide. Cut each strip across grain into ¼-inch-thick slices.

2. Add marinade to beef and mix well. Marinate at least 4 hours or overnight.

3. Combine ingredients for sauce. Mix well and set aside.

4. In a small Teflon frying pan, without oil, toast sesame seeds until golden brown (about 2 minutes).

5. In wok, heat oil to 325°. Add beaten egg white to meat. Mix thoroughly. Coat beef thoroughly with ¾ cup cornstarch. Drop beef into hot oil. Deep-fry for 4 minutes.

(continued)

105

6. While meat is frying, heat a saucepan. Add 1 tbsp. oil and chopped garlic. Stir-fry for 30 seconds. Add sauce from step 3. Bring quickly to a boil. Stir in thickening mixture. Cook for 30 seconds. Keep hot.

7. When meat has finished cooking, remove from oil and drain on paper towels. Place on a serving platter, pour hot sauce over, and sprinkle with toasted sesame seeds. Serve.

Advance preparation: Step 4 may be done up to a week ahead and sesame seeds stored in an airtight container at room temperature. Steps 1 and 2 may be done night before and refrigerated. Step 3 and thickening mixture may be prepared a few hours ahead and kept at room temperature.

Serving suggestion: Serve with Sweet Corn Soup, Siu Mai Dumplings, and Steamed Rice.

STEAK CUBES CHINESE STYLE
菜遠士的球

Serves 6

1 lb.	flank steak (makes about forty 1½-by-1-inch pieces)
1 lb.	broccoli
3½ tbsp.	oil
½ tsp.	salt
½ tsp.	sugar
½ cup	chicken stock
2 cloves	garlic, crushed
8 whole	dried red chili peppers
2	green onions, slivered

MARINADE

½ tsp.	baking soda
1 tsp.	warm water
½ tsp.	salt
½ tsp.	sugar
2 tsp.	dark soy sauce
1 tsp.	thin soy sauce
1 tbsp.	oyster sauce
1 tbsp.	cornstarch
Dash	pepper
2 tsp.	sesame oil
1½ tbsp.	white wine
2 cloves	garlic, finely chopped

THICKENING MIXTURE

2 tsp.	cornstarch mixed well with
2 tsp.	cold water
1 tsp.	dark soy sauce

1. Cut flank steak (with grain of meat) into 3 equal strips about 1½ inches wide. Cut each strip across grain slant-

wise into ¼-inch-thick slices. Slices must be thin! (See page 10.) Pieces will be about 1½ inches long and 1 inch wide.

2. To make marinade mix baking soda with warm water. Add to beef (this helps to tenderize the meat), then sprinkle on remaining ingredients. Mix well. Marinate overnight (or at least 5 hours).

3. Peel off outer, tough part of broccoli stalks. Cut stalks in half, then cut diagonally into slices ⅓ inch thick and about 1½ inches long. Cut flowerettes diagonally into 1½-inch pieces.

4. Heat wok and add 1 tbsp. oil and broccoli. Stir-fry for 2 minutes over high heat.

5. Add ½ tsp. salt, ½ tsp. sugar, and chicken stock. Cook uncovered for 2 minutes over high heat.

6. Stir in thickening mixture. Cook for 30 seconds over high heat. Remove from wok and set aside in a warm oven.

7. Heat wok and add 2½ tbsp. oil. Stir-fry garlic for 1 minute.

8. Add whole red chili peppers and beef. Stir-fry for 3 minutes over high heat. (If meat is not sufficiently cooked, increase cooking time.) Remove and discard garlic and red peppers.

9. Add slivered green onion and mix well.

10. Place broccoli on serving platter, then add beef as a topping. Serve.

Advance preparation: Steps 1 through 3 may be done a few hours ahead and kept at room temperature.

Serving suggestion: Serve with Deep-fried Squid, Princess Chicken, and Steamed Rice.

Variations: Asparagus or bok choy may be substituted for the broccoli, using the same cooking time. Snow peas may also be used, reducing the cooking time in step 4 to 1 minute, and in step 5 to 30 seconds.

SZECHUAN SPICED BEEF
川辣牛肉

1 lb.	flank steak
1 piece	Szechuan preserved radish* (to make ⅓ cup)
1 cup	warm water
20	snow peas
½ can	bamboo shoots* (about ¾ cup sliced)
1½ tbsp.	bean sauce**
1 tsp.	sugar
3 tbsp.	oil
2 tsp.	finely chopped garlic
9 whole	dried red chili peppers***
¾ cup	chicken stock
3	green onions, slivered
1½ tbsp.	sesame oil

MARINADE

½ tsp.	baking soda
1 tsp.	warm water
2 tsp.	sugar
1 tsp.	salt
2 tsp.	thin soy sauce
1 tsp.	dark soy sauce
2 tsp.	oyster sauce
1 tbsp.	white wine
1 tbsp.	cornstarch
Dash	pepper

THICKENING MIXTURE

1 tsp.	cornstarch mixed well with
2 tsp.	cold water

1. Cut flank steak lengthwise (with grain of meat) into 3 equal strips about 1½ inches wide. Cut each strip across grain into thin slices.

2. To make marinade, mix baking soda with warm water. Add to beef. Sprinkle on the rest of marinade ingredients. Mix and marinate overnight (or at least 4 hours).

3. Rinse preserved radish, then cut into thin strips. Soak in 1 cup warm water for 30 minutes. Rinse and drain.

4. Remove tips from snow peas. Cut peas diagonally into ¾-inch pieces.

5. Cut bamboo shoots into thin strips, julienne style.

6. Mash bean sauce into a paste with butt of a cleaver, add 1 tsp. sugar, and mix well.

7. Heat wok and add 1 tbsp. oil. Stir-fry bamboo shoots, preserved radish, and snow peas for 1 minute over medium heat. Remove from wok and set aside.

8. Heat wok. Add 2 tbsp. oil, chopped garlic, and chili peppers. Stir-fry for 30 seconds. Add beef and stir-fry for 3 minutes over high heat.

9. Add bean sauce mixture. Mix well.

10. Add chicken stock. Bring to a fast boil over high heat. (Be sure to stir and turn the beef to make sure it is cooking evenly.) Remove and discard chili peppers, or leave in if you prefer.

11. Add snow pea mixture and green onions. Toss well.

12. Stir in thickening mixture. Cook for 30 seconds.

13. Add sesame oil, mix well, and serve.

Advance preparation: Steps 1 through 7 may be done a few hours in advance and stored at room temperature.

Serving suggestion: Serve with Jennie's Noodle Soup, Eggplant Szechuan Style, and Steamed Rice.

*See Glossary, page 193.

**Use Cantonese-style bean sauce (Koon Chun brand). See Glossary.

***If you use 9 whole chili peppers, this dish will be quite spicy. You may adjust the seasoning to suit your own taste.

CHINESE BARBECUED PORK
叉燒

1 lb.	lean pork shoulder (butt) *or* pork loin		2 tsp.	thin soy sauce
2 cups	water (for roasting)		½ tsp.	roasting salt*
			1½ tsp.	oyster sauce
MARINADE			1½ tsp.	hoisin sauce
¼ tsp.	salt		2 tsp.	white wine
Dash	pepper		1 tbsp.	honey
1¼ tbsp.	sugar			

1. Cut meat into 1-inch-thick slices about 5-by-2 inches.

2. Combine ingredients for marinade. Marinate meat in this mixture at least 5 hours or overnight, in the refrigerator.

3. Preheat oven to 375°.

4. Put 2 cups water in a roasting pan and add any remaining marinade. (This helps keep meat moist.) Place a rack in pan and put meat on rack. Roast for 30 minutes on each side (total cooking time 1 hour), basting 3 or 4 times with juices from pan. (Do not cover.) Increase oven temperature to 425° and roast 10 minutes more (on one side only) to brown meat.

Advance preparation: The pork must marinate for at least 5 hours, but it can be marinated for as long as 2 days in the refrigerator.

Serving suggestion: To serve as an hors d'oeuvre, cut into 1½-inch by 1-inch slices. Use as a filling for sandwiches or as an ingredient in many dishes.

Note: Barbecued pork can be frozen for 3 months or refrigerated for 1 week.

*Roasting salt is necessary for both flavor and red color in this recipe. See Glossary.

CHINESE BARBECUED SPARERIBS
燒排骨

Serves 5

2 lb.	pork spareribs		1 tbsp.	thin soy sauce
2 cups	water (for roasting)		⅛ tsp.	five-spice powder* (optional)
1 tbsp.	honey for glaze		1 tsp.	roasting salt**
			1 tbsp.	oyster sauce
MARINADE			1 tbsp.	hoisin sauce
½ tsp.	salt		1 tbsp.	white wine
Dash	pepper		2 tbsp.	honey
2 tbsp.	sugar			

1. Have your butcher cut slab of spareribs in half across ribs.

2. Combine marinade ingredients. Marinate spareribs overnight (or at least 5 hours) in the refrigerator.

3. Preheat oven to 375°.

4. Put 2 cups water in a roasting pan (this helps keep meat moist and juicy) along with any remaining marinade. Place a rack in pan and put spareribs on rack. Roast 30 minutes on each side (total cooking time 1 hour). Do not cover. Baste 3 or 4 times during cooking, using juices in pan. After 1 hour, increase oven temperature to 425° and roast 10 minutes more, on one side only, to brown meat.

5. Remove from oven. Immediately glaze on both sides with 1 tbsp. honey. Cut apart into individual ribs. Serve.

Advance preparation: The entire recipe may be prepared a few hours in advance and kept at room temperature. Reheat, uncovered, at 350° for 10 minutes.

Serving suggestion: Spareribs may be served as an hors d'oeuvre or may be accompanied with almost any dish.

*See Glossary.

**In this recipe, you must use roasting salt, for both flavor and color. See Glossary.

JENNIE'S STEAMED PORK CAKE
蒸豬肉餅

6 small	(about 2 tbsp. chopped) Chinese mushrooms (dried)	
1 small	dried squid* (optional) (about 2 tbsp. chopped)	
8	dried shrimp	
1½ tbsp.	Tientsin preserved vegetables,** rinsed	
1 lb.	lean ground pork**	
2	green onions, finely chopped	
1	egg	

SEASONING

1 tsp.	salt
1½ tsp.	sugar
1 tsp.	thin soy sauce
1 tsp.	dark soy sauce
2 tsp.	oyster sauce
1 tbsp.	white wine
1½ tbsp.	cornstarch
1½ tbsp.	cold water
Dash	pepper

1. Boil Chinese mushrooms in water to cover for 10 minutes. Rinse, drain, and squeeze dry. Cut off and discard stems. Chop mushrooms fine.

2. Soak squid and shrimp for 15 minutes in warm water to cover. Rinse and drain. Peel off and discard skin from squid. Chop squid and shrimp into very small pieces.

3. Combine mushrooms, squid, shrimp, preserved vegetables, ground pork, and green onions on chopping board. Chop and mix until well combined (about 20 strokes). You may use a food processor for this. Place mixture in a shallow dish or pie pan.

4. Beat egg lightly with a fork. Add to meat mixture and mix thoroughly. Sprinkle on seasoning and mix again. Flatten to make a thick pancake.

5. Using a wok or steamer, steam for 25 minutes over high heat. (See "Steaming," p. 7.)

Advance preparation: Steps 1 through 4 may be done a few hours ahead. Keep refrigerated or at room temperature until ready to steam.

Serving suggestion: Serve with Chicken with Chili Peppers, Beef with Bok Choy, and Steamed Rice.

*Dried squid is optional in this recipe, but the flavor of the dish is definitely improved when it is included. Leftover squid may be kept at room temperature in a dry place for 2 years.

**See Glossary.

MO SHU PORK
木樨肉薄餅

MANDARIN PANCAKES FOR MO SHU PORK   Makes 6

1½ cups all-purpose flour
½ cup   boiling water
2 tbsp. cold water

3 tbsp.   oil (approximately)
Sesame oil

1. Sift flour into a mixing bowl. Gradually add boiling water and stir with chopsticks. Add cold water and mix well.

2. Using your hands, shape dough into a ball. Knead until smooth (approximately 1 minute). Cover with damp cloth for 20 minutes.

3. Flour board and knead dough for 1 minute. Form dough into a long strip. Cut into 6 equal pieces.

4. Flatten each piece with palm of hand, then roll out to circles 7 inches in diameter.

5. Lightly brush top of 1 pancake with sesame oil and place another pancake on top. (Pancakes for Mo Shu Pork are cooked together in pairs to obtain a softness rather than a crispy texture. Sesame oil aids in separating pancakes after cooking.)

6. Heat a Teflon or cast iron skillet over medium heat. Lightly coat skillet with oil. (Be sure to heat skillet sufficiently, or pancake will stick.) Add paired pancakes, cover skillet, and cook for 1½ minutes. Top pancake should bubble slightly, and bottom pancake will have light golden brown spots. Flip pancake, cover, and cook until light brown (approximately 45 seconds).

7. Remove from skillet. Separate 2 pancakes. Wrap in foil and place in a warm oven. Repeat the entire process with remaining pancakes.

(continued)   113

Advance preparation: Cooked pancakes will keep for several days in the refrigerator, or may be frozen up to 3 months. If refrigerated, reheat by steaming for 5 minutes. If frozen, steam without thawing for 7 minutes.

Variation: Flour tortillas may be used in place of mandarin pancakes. Steam for 3 minutes to heat.

MO SHU PORK FILLING
木樨肉

Serves 6 (6 pancakes)

2 pieces	dried black fungus* (about ½ cup after soaking and cutting into slivers)
½ lb.	pork butt
½ lb.	spinach (about 2 cups cut up) (or snow peas, Napa cabbage, or cabbage)
2½ tsp.	bean sauce**
3½ tbsp.	oil
2	eggs, beaten with a fork
Sprinkle	salt
Sprinkle	sugar
1 tbsp.	sesame oil
1 recipe	Mandarin Pancakes

SEASONING

½ tsp.	salt
½ tsp.	sugar
1 tsp.	thin soy sauce
1 tsp.	oyster sauce
2 tsp.	white wine
2 tsp.	cornstarch
Dash	pepper

CONDIMENT

2 tbsp.	hoisin sauce
3	green onions (white part only), slivered

1. Soak black fungus for 15 minutes in warm water to cover. Rinse thoroughly. Remove and discard stems. Cut fungus into slivers.

2. Trim excess fat from pork butt. Cut pork into thin strips julienne style. Sprinkle on seasoning and mix well.

3. Wash spinach thoroughly. Remove stems and cut spinach into 2-inch pieces. (If using snow peas, Napa cabbage, or cabbage, cut into julienne strips.)

4. Mash bean sauce into a paste with butt of a cleaver.

5. Heat wok and add 1 tbsp. oil. Scramble eggs, remove from wok, and set aside.

114

6. Heat wok and add 1 tbsp. oil. Stir-fry spinach and black fungus for 1 minute over high heat, sprinkling lightly with salt and sugar. Remove from wok and set aside.

7. Heat wok and add 1½ tbsp. oil. Stir-fry pork for 2 minutes over high heat. Add bean sauce and mix well. Add chicken stock, cover, and cook over high heat for 3 minutes. Pour off all liquid.

8. Add spinach mixture, eggs, and sesame oil. Mix well.

9. Each person rolls his own pancake and eats it like a burrito: Spread 1 tsp. hoisin sauce in the center of the pancake. Add a few slivers of green onion, then add 3 tbsp. meat mixture.

Fold left side toward center, 1 inch from the edge. (This fold keeps the juices from dripping out.)

Roll up from the bottom to the top. Eat like a burrito.

Advance preparation: Steps 1 through 7 may be done a few hours in advance and kept at room temperature.

Serving suggestion: Mo Shu Pork with Mandarin Pancakes is served as a first course and goes well with any dish. Mo Shu Pork mixture may also be served without pancakes if desired.

*See Glossary, page 188.

**Use Cantonese-style bean sauce (Koon Chun brand), not Szechuan hot bean sauce. See Glossary.

PORK WITH MUSHROOMS AND MUSTARD GREENS
蠔油冬菇扒芥菜

Serves 6

2 oz.	(about 40) small Chinese mushrooms (dried)
1 qt.	warm water
½ lb.	pork butt
3	green onions
1 lb.	Chinese mustard greens*
1 tbsp.	oil
1 tbsp.	white wine
1 tsp.	sugar
3 cups	chicken stock
1 slice	ginger (1-inch diameter) 1 inch thick, crushed
1 qt.	water
1½ tbsp.	oyster sauce
1 tsp.	dark soy sauce

SEASONING

½ tsp.	salt
½ tsp.	sugar
1½ tsp.	thin soy sauce
1½ tsp.	cornstarch
Dash	pepper

THICKENING MIXTURE

1 tbsp.	cornstarch mixed well with
2 tbsp.	cold water

1. Soak mushrooms in 1 qt. warm water for 30 minutes. Rinse, squeeze dry, and cut off and discard stems. Leave mushrooms whole.

2. Trim fat from pork. Cut into ¼-inch-thick slices about 1½-by-½ inch. Sprinkle on seasoning and mix well.

3. Cut off white part of green onion. Cut into slivers and reserve for garnishing dish. Leave green part whole for cooking.

4. Remove outer leaves of mustard greens and trim ends. Peel off tough outer covering of center stalk and discard. Cut stalk in half lengthwise. Cut stalk and leaves diagonally into 2-inch pieces.

5. Heat wok and add 1 tbsp. oil. Add mushrooms. Stir-fry for 2 minutes over medium heat. Add wine, sugar, chicken stock, ginger, and whole green onion tops. Bring to a fast boil, cover, and cook over medium heat for 1 hour. Stir occasionally and be sure there is enough liquid. After cooking, there should be 1 cup of liquid remaining. (If not, add more chicken stock.) Remove and discard ginger and green onion tops.

6. Add seasoned pork, cover, and cook for 5 minutes over high heat.

7. While pork is cooking, bring 1 qt. water to a boil. Add mustard greens and cook uncovered for 3 minutes. (Start timing immediately. Do not wait until water returns to a boil.) Remove, drain, and place on serving platter.

8. Add oyster sauce and dark soy sauce to cooked pork and mushroom mixture in step 6.

9. Stir in thickening mixture and cook for 30 seconds. Pour mixture over bed of mustard greens. Garnish with slivered green onions.

Advance preparation: Steps 1 through 6 can be prepared as long as 2 days ahead and refrigerated, or several hours in advance and kept at room temperature. Reheat pork and mushroom mixture and complete steps 7 through 9.

Serving suggestion: Serve with Braised Fish in Hot Bean Sauce and Steamed Rice.

Variation: Broccoli, asparagus, or snow peas may be substituted for mustard greens. Use the same cooking time for broccoli and asparagus. Snow peas require only 1 minute of parboiling.

*Not the same as "American" mustard greens. See Glossary, page 190.

SPICED PORK
辣肉片

Serves 6

1 lb.	pork butt
2	carrots
2 stalks	celery
1	green bell pepper *or*
	20 snow peas
3 tbsp.	oil
½ cup	sliced fresh mushrooms
2	green onions, slivered
½ tsp.	salt
½ tsp.	sugar
2 tsp.	finely chopped garlic
8 whole	dried red chili peppers (optional)
1 cup	chicken stock
1½ tbsp.	hoisin sauce

SEASONING

1 tsp.	salt
1½ tsp.	sugar
1 tsp.	thin soy sauce
1 tsp.	dark soy sauce
1 tsp.	oyster sauce
1 tbsp.	white wine
1 tbsp.	cornstarch
Dash	pepper

THICKENING MIXTURE

2 tsp.	cornstarch mixed well with
1 tbsp.	cold water
1 tbsp.	sesame oil

1. Cut pork into ¼-inch-thick slices about 1-by-½ inch. Sprinkle seasoning on pork and mix well.

2. Peel and cut carrots diagonally into thin slices.

3. Remove celery strings with a vegetable peeler and cut celery into 1½-inch pieces, then cut each piece lengthwise into strips, julienne style.

4. Remove seeds from bell pepper, then cut into pieces about 1-by-½ inch. If you use snow peas, remove tips and cut peas diagonally into 1-inch pieces.

5. Heat wok and add 1 tbsp. oil, carrots, fresh mushrooms, celery, green pepper or snow peas, and green onions. Stir-fry for 1 minute over high heat, sprinkling with ½ tsp. salt and ½ tsp. sugar. Remove from wok and set aside.

6. Heat wok. Add 2 tbsp. oil, chopped garlic, and whole chili peppers. Stir-fry for 30 seconds over high heat. Add pork and stir-fry for 3 minutes.

7. Add chicken stock, cover, and cook for 4 minutes. Remove and discard chili pepper.

8. Add hoisin sauce. Mix well.

9. Add cooked vegetables and toss well.

10. Stir in thickening mixture. Cook for 30 seconds and serve.

Advance preparation: Steps 1 through 7 and thickening mixture can be prepared a few hours ahead and kept at room temperature until ready to complete the dish.

Serving suggestion: Serve with Asparagus in Oyster Sauce, Prawns with Lobster Sauce, and Steamed Rice.

STEAMED MINCED PORK WITH SALTED FISH
鹹魚蒸肉餅

Serves 4

½ lb.	lean ground pork*		1 tsp.	sugar
1	green onion, finely chopped		2 tsp.	white wine
1 large	egg, lightly beaten with fork		1 tsp.	thin soy sauce
1 piece	salted fish** (3-by-1 inch)		1 tsp.	oyster sauce
1 tsp.	slivered ginger		2 tsp.	cornstarch
			2 tsp.	cold water
SEASONING			Dash	pepper
½ tsp.	salt			

1. Combine ground pork and chopped green onion on a chopping board. Using a cleaver, chop and mix until well combined (about 20 strokes). A food processor may be used for this step. Put mixture in an 8-inch shallow china dish or pie plate.

(continued)

2. Sprinkle seasoning on ground pork mixture. Mix well. Add beaten egg. Mix well again. Flatten into a thick pan-cake.

3. Rinse salted fish and cut into 1-inch pieces. Place on top of ground pork mixture.

4. Add slivered ginger on top of salted fish.

5. Using a wok or steamer (see "Steaming," page 7), steam for 25 minutes over high heat.

Advance preparation: Steps 1 through 4 may be done a few hours ahead. Refrigerate.

Serving suggestion: This dish should be served with Steamed Rice.

*See Glossary.

**Salted fish usually comes whole, and you must cut it into pieces yourself. Do not let its odor deter you; after being rinsed, then steamed with ginger, it loses its strong odor. It is a great favorite with Oriental people, and the adventurous diner should sample it at least once. The fish alone may be steamed with slivered ginger and 1 tbsp. oil and eaten with rice.

STEAMED PORK CAKE WITH SALTED DUCK EGGS
鹹蛋蒸肉餅

Serves 6

1 lb.	lean ground pork*		1 tsp.	sugar
1	green onion, finely chopped		1 tsp.	thin soy sauce
2	salted duck eggs*		1 tsp.	dark soy sauce
1 large	egg		2 tsp.	oyster sauce
			1 tbsp.	white wine
SEASONING			1 tbsp.	cornstarch
¾ tsp.	salt		Dash	pepper

1. Place ground pork and chopped green onion on chopping board. Mix and chop for approximately 20 strokes. Put mixture in an 8-inch shallow dish or pie pan.

2. Sprinkle seasoning on ground pork mixture and mix well.

3. Remove black coating from duck eggs. Discard one egg white and place the other in a bowl (using both duck egg whites will make this dish too salty). Cut each duck egg yolk into 4 pieces.

4. To duck egg white, add 1 large egg. Beat lightly with a fork. Add to meat mixture and mix thoroughly. Flatten into a thick pancake.

5. Place pieces of duck egg yolk on top of meat mixture.

6. Using a wok or steamer (see "Steaming," p. 7), steam for 25 minutes over high heat. Serve.

Advance preparation: Steps 1 through 5 may be done a few hours ahead and refrigerated until ready to steam.

Serving suggestion: This dish should be served with Steamed Rice.

*See Glossary.

STEAMED SPARERIBS WITH BLACK BEAN SAUCE
豆豉蒸排骨

Serves 4

1½ lb.	spareribs	2 tsp.	dark soy sauce
2 tsp.	finely chopped garlic	2 tsp.	oyster sauce
2	green onions, finely chopped	1 tbsp.	white wine
2 tbsp.	salted black beans*	1 tbsp.	cornstarch
		1 tbsp.	cold water
SEASONING		2 tsp.	sesame oil
1 tsp.	salt	Dash	pepper
2 tsp.	sugar		

1. Have your butcher cut the spareribs into strips 1½ inches wide. At home, cut the rib bones apart and trim off fat.

2. Place spareribs in an 8-inch shallow dish or pie pan. Sprinkle on seasoning and mix well. Add chopped garlic and chopped green onion.

(continued)

3. Wash black beans twice. Drain and set aside.

4. Steam spareribs for 15 minutes over high heat (see "Steaming," p. 7). Stir so that top layer is turned to bottom, to let spareribs cook evenly. Add black beans and steam for 15 minutes more. Serve.

Advance preparation: Steps 1 through 3 may be done a few hours ahead and refrigerated until ready to steam.

Serving suggestion: Serve with West Lake Minced Beef Soup, Minced Oysters with Lettuce Leaves, and Steamed Rice.

Variation: Pork butt or pork tenderloin may be prepared this way also. Cut into 1½-inch cubes and proceed as above.

*Salted black beans come in a plastic bag or a box, labeled "Salty Black Beans." See Glossary, page 185.

SWEET AND SOUR PORK CHOPS
甜酸猪排

Serves 4

4	boneless pork chops (about 1 lb.)
½ can	baby corn ears* ("mini-corn") or 1 small can pineapple, chunk style (drained)
1	carrot
1	green bell pepper
1 stalk	celery
1 qt.	oil for deep-frying
1 tbsp.	oil for stir-frying
¼ tsp.	salt
¼ tsp.	sugar

SEASONING MIXTURE

¾ tsp.	salt
¾ tsp.	sugar
1 ½ tsp.	thin soy sauce
1 ½ tsp.	white wine
Dash	pepper

COATING MIXTURE

¼ cup	Bisquick
¼ cup	cornstarch
2 tbsp.	tapioca starch*

SWEET AND SOUR SAUCE

¾ cup	water
6 tbsp.	cider vinegar
3 tbsp.	catsup
⅓ tsp.	salt
¾ tsp.	thin soy sauce
6 tbsp.	sugar

THICKENING MIXTURE

1 ¼ tbsp.	cornstarch mixed well with
2 tbsp.	cold water

1. Place pork chops on a chopping board. With flat side of a cleaver, pound each pork chop several times to tenderize. Cut into 2-by-1-inch strips.

2. Add seasoning mixture to pork strips and mix well.

3. Cut baby corn diagonally into 1-inch pieces.

4. Peel carrot and cut diagonally into very thin slices.

5. Cut bell pepper in half. Remove and discard seeds. Cut each pepper half into 1-by-½-inch pieces.

6. Peel celery with vegetable peeler. Cut crosswise into 1½-inch pieces, then cut each piece lengthwise into strips, julienne style.

7. Combine ingredients for coating mixture and mix well.

(continued)

123

8. Heat 1 qt. oil in wok to 325°. Coat pork strips with coating mixture and drop into hot oil. Deep-fry for 5 minutes. Remove pork from oil and drain on paper towels. Remove oil from wok.

9. Heat wok and add 1 tbsp. oil, baby corn, carrot, bell pepper, and celery. (If using pineapple, add in step 12. Do not stir-fry!) Stir-fry for 2 minutes. Sprinkle with ¼ tsp. salt and ¼ tsp. sugar. Remove from wok and set aside.

10. Mix ingredients for Sweet and Sour Sauce and bring to a boil.

11. Stir in thickening mixture. Cook for 1 minute.

12. Add vegetable mixture, deep-fried pork strips, and pineapple. Mix well. (Do not overcook! Heat through only.) Serve.

Advance preparation: Steps 1 through 9 may be done a few hours ahead and kept at room temperature.

Serving suggestion: Serve with Beef with Asparagus, Butterfly Prawns, and Steamed Rice.

*See Glossary.

MONGOLIAN LAMB
蒙古羊肉

Serves 4

½ lb.	lamb shoulder (or leg)	¼ cup	chicken stock
15	snow peas	½ tbsp.	sesame oil
2 cups	oil for deep-frying		
1 oz.	rice sticks*	**SEASONING**	
1½ tbsp.	oil for stir-frying	½ tsp.	salt
1 tsp.	finely chopped garlic	1 tsp.	sugar
1 tsp.	finely chopped ginger	1 tsp.	thin soy sauce
½ tsp.	crushed dried red chili pepper	1 tsp.	oyster sauce
2	green onions, slivered	1 tbsp.	white wine
2 tsp.	hoisin sauce	2 tsp.	cornstarch
		Dash	pepper

124

1. Cut lamb into ¼-inch-thick slices about 1½-by-½ inch.

2. Sprinkle seasoning on lamb and mix well.

3. Remove tips from snow peas. Cut peas diagonally into ½-inch pieces.

4. Heat 2 cups oil to 325° in a wok. Drop in a piece of rice stick to test oil temperature. (It should puff up immediately. If not, heat the oil a little longer.) Drop half of rice sticks into oil. They should immediately puff up. Turn over and deep-fry the other side if necessary. Remove to paper towels to drain excess oil. Repeat with remainder of rice sticks. Break fried rice sticks into approximately 2-inch lengths. Set aside. Remove oil from wok.

5. Heat wok and add 1½ tbsp. oil. Add garlic and ginger. Stir-fry for 30 seconds over high heat. Add crushed chili pepper and lamb. Stir-fry for 3 minutes.

6. Add snow peas and green onion. Toss well. Add hoisin sauce and chicken stock. Mix thoroughly. Cook uncovered for 2 minutes over high heat.

7. Add sesame oil. Mix well. Remove to serving platter. Sprinkle rice sticks over top. (They don't need to be hot.) Serve immediately.

Advance preparation: Step 4 may be done several days ahead and the rice sticks stored in an airtight container. Steps 1 through 3 may be done several hours ahead and stored at room temperature.

Serving suggestion: Serve with Spinach Soup, Whole Fresh Crab in Curry Sauce, and Steamed Rice.

*Rice sticks are called py mei fun. For deep-frying, buy the variety that comes in a parchmentlike wrapping (those in the plastic bag do not deep fry as well). There are also rice sticks called lai fun, which are used in soups. Be careful to choose the right kind. See Glossary.

FISH AND SHELLFISH

BRAISED FISH IN HOT BEAN SAUCE
原豉醬乾燒魚

1½ lb.	piece rock cod, about 1¼ inch thick, or filet, about ¾ inch thick (or sea bass, salmon, sturgeon, or other firm fish)
½ tsp.	salt
2½ tbsp.	cornstarch
4 tbsp.	oil
1½ tbsp.	hot bean sauce*
1 tsp.	sugar
1 tsp.	finely chopped ginger
2 tsp.	finely chopped garlic
2	green onions, finely chopped
1 tbsp.	sesame oil

SAUCE

1 cup	chicken stock
2 tbsp.	white wine
2 tsp.	sugar
1 tbsp.	oyster sauce
1 tbsp.	dark soy sauce
Dash	pepper

THICKENING MIXTURE

2 tsp.	cornstarch mixed well with
2 tsp.	cold water

1. Rinse fish and drain thoroughly. Sprinkle fish with ½ tsp. salt and coat with 2½ tbsp. cornstarch. (This should be done just before pan-frying.)

2. Heat wok or frying pan. Add 3 tbsp. oil. Pan-fry fish, skin side down, over medium heat for 3 minutes. Turn and fry opposite side for 3 minutes. Then fry each cut side for 2 minutes (total cooking time 10 minutes). (If using a filet, pan-fry for 2 minutes; turn and fry other side for 2 minutes.) Remove from wok and set aside.

3. Mash hot bean sauce into a paste with butt of a cleaver. Add 1 tsp. sugar and mix well.

4. Combine ingredients for sauce. Mix well and set aside.

5. Heat wok. Add 1 tbsp. oil, chopped ginger, and garlic. Stir-fry for 30 seconds over high heat. Add hot bean sauce, fish, green onions, and sauce. Bring to a fast boil. Cover and cook for 3 minutes. Turn and cook for 2 minutes more. (Total cooking time for a filet is 3 minutes; no need to turn.)

6. Stir thickening mixture into gravy. Cook for 30 seconds.

7. Sprinkle sesame oil over fish and serve.

Advance preparation: Steps 1 through 4 may be done a few hours ahead and kept at room temperature.

Serving suggestion: Serve with Broccoli with Barbecued Pork, Beef with Fresh Bean Cake, and Steamed Rice.

*Szechuan type. If a less spicy dish is desired, use Cantonese-style bean sauce (Koon Chun brand). See Glossary.

BRAISED FISH IN TOMATO SAUCE
番茄炆魚
Serves 6

1½ lb.	rock cod steak about 1½ inch thick, or filet about ¾ inch thick (or sea bass, salmon, sturgeon, or other firm fish)
1 tsp.	salt
2½ tbsp.	cornstarch
4 tbsp.	oil
1 slice	fresh ginger (1-inch diameter) ½ inch thick, crushed
6	medium-sized tomatoes (about 1 lb.)
¼ cup	chopped yellow onion
1	green onion, finely chopped

SAUCE

3 tbsp.	catsup
1½ tbsp.	cider vinegar
¼ cup	chicken stock
1 tbsp.	white wine
1 tbsp.	sugar
¼ tsp.	salt
1 tsp.	thin soy sauce

THICKENING MIXTURE

2 tsp.	cornstarch mixed well with
4 tsp.	cold water

(continued)

1. Rinse fish and drain thoroughly. Sprinkle salt over surface. Rub cornstarch onto all surfaces. (This should be done just before pan-frying fish.)

2. Heat wok or frying pan. Add 3 tbsp. oil and crushed ginger. Cook for 30 seconds. Add fish, skin side down, and pan-fry for 3 minutes over medium heat. Turn and fry opposite side for 3 minutes. Then fry each cut side for 2 minutes (total cooking time 10 minutes). For a filet, pan-fry for 2 minutes; turn and fry other side for 2 minutes.

3. Remove fish from wok and set aside. Discard ginger.

4. Cut tomatoes in half; cut each half into 4 wedges.

5. Combine ingredients for sauce. Mix well. Set aside.

6. Heat wok. Add 1 tbsp. oil, chopped yellow onion, and tomatoes. Stir-fry for 30 seconds over high heat. Add pan-fried fish and sauce mixture. Bring quickly to fast boil, cover, and cook for 3 minutes over high heat. Turn fish and cook for 2 minutes more. (Total cooking time for a filet is 3 minutes; no need to turn.)

7. Stir thickening mixture into gravy and cook for 30 seconds. Garnish with chopped green onion. Serve.

Advance preparation: Steps 1 through 5 may be done a few hours ahead and kept at room temperature.

Serving suggestion: This dish is usually served with Steamed Rice.

BRAISED FISH WITH BLACK BEAN SAUCE
豉汁炆魚

Serves 6

1½ lb.	piece rock cod about 1½ inches thick, *or* filet about ¾ inch thick (*or* sea bass, salmon, sturgeon, *or* other firm fish)
½ tsp.	salt
2½ tbsp.	cornstarch
4 tbsp.	oil
2 tbsp.	salted black beans*
2 tsp.	finely chopped ginger
2 tsp.	finely chopped garlic
2	green onions, finely chopped

SAUCE

1½ tbsp.	white wine
1 cup	chicken stock
2 tsp.	oyster sauce
1 tsp.	dark soy sauce
1 tsp.	thin soy sauce
2½ tsp.	sugar
Dash	pepper

THICKENING MIXTURE

2 tsp.	cornstarch mixed well with
4 tsp.	cold water

1. Rinse fish and drain thoroughly. Sprinkle salt over surface. Rub cornstarch onto all surfaces. (Do this just before frying fish.)

2. Heat wok or frying pan. Add 3 tbsp. oil. Pan-fry fish, skin side down, for 3 minutes over medium heat. Turn and fry opposite side for 3 minutes. Then fry each cut side for 2 minutes (total cooking time 10 minutes). (For a filet, pan-fry for 2 minutes, then turn and fry other side 2 minutes.) Remove from wok and set aside.

3. Wash black beans twice. Drain. Mash into a paste with butt of a cleaver. Add chopped ginger and garlic.

4. Combine ingredients for sauce. Mix well and set aside.

5. Heat wok. Add 1 tbsp. oil. Stir-fry black bean mixture for 30 seconds over high heat. Add pan-fried fish, sauce mixture, and chopped green onion. Bring to a fast boil and cover. Cook for 3 minutes. Turn fish and cook 2 minutes more. (Total cooking time for a filet is 3 minutes; no need to turn.)

6. Add thickening mixture and cook for 30 seconds. Serve.

(continued)

129

Advance preparation: Steps 1 through 4 may be done a few hours ahead. Keep at room temperature.

Serving suggestion: Serve with Eggplant Szechuan Style, Deep-fried Chicken Wings, and Steamed Rice.

Variation: If a spicier sauce is desired, add 1 tsp. crushed dried red chili pepper to the black bean mixture in step 3.

*These come in a package or box labeled "Salty Black Beans." See Glossary, page 185.

EIGHT FLAVORS STEAMED FISH
八寶蒸石斑

Serves 4

10	small Chinese mushrooms (dried)
20	pieces lily flowers*
2 cups	warm water
2	dried red dates**
1½ tbsp.	Tientsin preserved vegetables*** (rinse and drain)
1½ lb.	rock cod steak, about 1¼ inches thick, or filet, about ¾ inch thick (or sea bass, salmon, sturgeon, or other firm fish)
2	green onions, slivered
1½ tsp.	slivered ginger
¼ cup	sliced Chinese Barbecued Pork, page 110, or bacon
½ tsp.	salt
¾ tsp.	sugar
1 tbsp.	dark soy sauce
2 tsp.	oyster sauce
1 tbsp.	white wine
Dash	pepper
1½ tbsp.	oil
½ tbsp.	sesame oil

1. Soak mushrooms and lily flowers in 1 cup warm water for 20 minutes. Rinse and squeeze dry. Remove and discard mushroom stems; cut mushrooms into strips julienne style. Cut ¼ inch off pointed end of each lily flower and discard. Cut each lily flower in half.

2. Soak red dates in 1 cup warm water for 7 minutes. Cut red dates in half and discard seeds. Cut dates in slivers.

3. Rinse fish and drain thoroughly. Place in an 8-inch shallow china dish or stainless steel pie plate. Sprinkle evenly with salt, sugar, dark soy sauce, oyster sauce, white wine, dash of pepper, oil, and sesame oil.

4. Garnish fish with mushrooms, lily flowers, red dates, preserved vegetables, green onions, ginger, and barbecued pork or bacon.

5. Using a wok or steamer (see "Steaming," p. 7), steam for approximately 20 minutes over high heat. Since some pieces of fish may be thicker than others, test for doneness by pressing gently with a chopstick. If chopstick penetrates fish easily, fish is done. (See note.) Serve.

Advance preparation: Steps 1 through 4 may be done a few hours in advance and refrigerated until ready to steam.

Serving suggestion: Serve with Minced Squab with Lettuce Leaves, Princess Chicken, and Steamed Rice.

Note: The steaming time (20 minutes) is approximately the correct amount of time for a piece of fish 1½ inches thick. If fish is 1 inch thick, steam for 15 minutes; if ½ inch thick, 10 minutes.

*Lily flowers are also called "golden needles." See Glossary.

**See Glossary, page 193.

***See Glossary, page 192.

FISH AND VEGETABLES IN BLACK BEAN SAUCE
豉汁魚片

½ lb.	filet of rock cod (with skin on, if possible)
2	green onions
1 stalk	celery
10	snow peas
1½ tbsp.	salted black beans*
½ tsp.	crushed dried red chili pepper**
1 tsp.	finely chopped garlic
2 tbsp.	oil
1 can	(6¾ oz.) button mushrooms, drained, *or* 1 cup sliced fresh mushrooms
¼ tsp.	salt
¼ tsp.	sugar
1 tbsp.	white wine
⅓ cup	chicken stock
1½ tsp.	sesame oil

SEASONING

⅓ tsp.	salt
1 tsp.	sugar
1 tsp.	thin soy sauce
1 tsp.	oyster sauce
Dash	pepper

THICKENING MIXTURE

1½ tsp.	cornstarch mixed well with
2 tsp.	cold water

1. Cut fish into ½-by-1-inch pieces. (Leave skin on. It holds fish together for stir-frying.)

2. Add seasoning to fish. Mix well.

3. Cut green onions into ¾-inch pieces.

4. Remove celery strings with a vegetable peeler. Cut celery into 2-inch pieces, then cut each piece lengthwise into ¼-inch strips, julienne style.

5. Remove tips from snow peas. Cut diagonally into pieces approximately 1½ inches wide.

6. Rinse black beans twice. Drain and mash into a paste with butt of a cleaver. Add crushed red chili pepper and chopped garlic. Mix well.

7. Heat wok. Add ½ tbsp. oil, button mushrooms, or fresh mushrooms, green onions, celery, and snow peas. Stir-fry for 1 minute over high heat. Sprinkle with ¼ tsp. salt and ¼ tsp. sugar. Remove from wok and set aside.

8. Heat wok. Add 1½ tbsp. oil, black bean mixture, and fish. Stir-fry for 1½ minutes over high heat. Add wine and chicken stock. Bring to a fast boil, uncovered.

9. Add vegetable mixture. Toss well.

10. Stir in thickening mixture. Cook for 30 seconds. Add sesame oil and mix well. Serve.

Advance preparation: Steps 1 through 7 may be done a few hours in advance and kept at room temperature.

Serving suggestion: Serve with Spiced Pork, Minced Squab with Lettuce Leaves, and Steamed Rice.

*See Glossary, page 185.

**Omit crushed red pepper if a less spicy dish is desired.

STEAMED RED SNAPPER
原豉醬蒸魚

Serves 4

¾ lb.	red snapper filets*
1 tbsp.	bean sauce**
2	green onions, diced
1 tsp.	slivered ginger
2 tbsp.	oil

SEASONING MIXTURE

¼ tsp.	salt
¼ tsp.	sugar
½ tsp.	thin soy sauce
1 tsp.	dark soy sauce

1 tsp.	oyster sauce
2 tsp.	white wine
Dash	pepper

1. Rinse fish, drain thoroughly, and place in an 8-inch shallow china dish or stainless steel pie plate.

2. Sprinkle fish evenly with seasoning mixture.

3. Mash bean sauce into a paste with butt of a cleaver. Spread on top of fish. Sprinkle diced green onions, slivered ginger, and oil over fish.

4. Using a wok or steamer (see "Steaming," p. 7), steam for 12 minutes over high heat.

(continued)

Advance preparation: Steps 1 through 3 may be done a few hours ahead. Keep in the refrigerator until ready to steam.

Serving suggestion: This dish should be served with Steamed Rice.

*Any firm-fleshed fish such as rock cod, sand dabs, Rex sole, or salmon can be substituted. The steaming time given is for filets approximately ¾ inch thick. Some filets are thicker and require longer cooking. Test for doneness by piercing thickest part of fish with a chopstick. If chopstick penetrates easily, fish is cooked.

**Cantonese-style bean sauce (Koon Chun brand). If you prefer spicy food, use Szechuan-style bean sauce. See Glossary.

STEAMED ROCK COD
蒸石斑

Serves 5

1½ lb.	piece of rock cod, about 1¼ inch thick (salmon, sea bass, or sturgeon could be used)	
2 tsp.	slivered ginger	
2	green onions, slivered	
3 tbsp.	oil	

SEASONING MIXTURE

1 tsp.	salt
1 tsp.	sugar
2 tsp.	dark soy sauce
2 tsp.	thin soy sauce
1 tbsp.	white wine
Dash	pepper

1. Rinse fish, drain thoroughly, and place in an 8-inch shallow china dish or stainless steel pie plate.

2. Sprinkle fish evenly with seasoning mixture. Sprinkle slivered ginger and slivered green onion over fish.

3. Using a wok or steamer (see "Steaming," p. 7), steam for 20 minutes over high heat. (Poke fish gently with chopstick. If chopstick penetrates easily, fish is cooked.)

4. Put oil in a small saucepan. About a minute before fish is done, heat oil for 1 minute over high heat.

5. Remove dish containing fish to counter. Immediately pour hot oil over the fish; the oil should be so hot it sizzles when it hits the fish. (The hot oil removes any "fishy" flavor.) Serve.

Advance preparation: Steps 1 and 2 may be done a few hours in advance and kept refrigerated until ready to steam.

Serving suggestion: Serve with Chicken and Snow Peas in Black Bean Sauce, Parchment Beef, and Steamed Rice.

Note: The steaming time given is based on fish 1¼ inches to 1½ inches thick. If fish is 1 inch thick, steam for 15 minutes; if only ½ inch thick, steam for 10 minutes.

BUTTERFLY PRAWNS
蝴蝶蝦

Serves 4

BATTER

1¾ tbsp.	water chestnut powder*	20	raw medium-sized prawns in shells
2 tbsp.	cold water	¼ tsp.	salt
1 tbsp.	oil	¼ tsp.	sugar
¼ tsp.	salt	Dash	pepper
¼ tsp.	(scant) baking soda	2 strips	thin bacon
1 large	egg white	6 tbsp.	tapioca starch**
		1 qt.	oil for deep-frying

1. To make batter, place water chestnut powder in a bowl. Add cold water and mix well. Add oil, salt, baking soda, and egg white. Mix thoroughly. Let stand at room temperature for 5 hours, or prepare day before and refrigerate overnight. (This activates baking soda.) Batter will be thin.

2. Shell prawns. Devein, cutting a little deeper than usual so that prawns may be pressed open like a butterfly. Wash and drain.

(continued)

3. Add ¼ tsp. salt, ¼ tsp. sugar, and dash pepper to prawns. Mix well.

4. Cut bacon into 1-inch lengths.

5. Place tapioca starch on a plate. Place a piece of bacon on cut side of a prawn. With bacon side down, press firmly into tapioca starch. Turn over and again press into tapioca starch. (It may be necessary to turn and press into tapioca starch several times to make sure bacon will stick to prawn.) Repeat with remaining prawns, adding more tapioca starch if necessary.

6. Heat oil to 325° in a wok. Stir batter. Dip each prawn into batter and let excess batter drip back into bowl. Immediately drop prawn into hot oil, stirring slightly to keep it from sticking to the bottom of wok. Deep-fry approximately 6 prawns at a time, for 2 minutes on each side (total cooking time 4 minutes). Remove and drain on paper towels. Repeat with remaining prawns. Serve.

Condiment: Use Hot Mustard (page 53) and catsup as condiments.

Advance preparation: Steps 1 through 4 may be done in advance. Store in the refrigerator until ready to use.

Serving suggestion: Serve as an appetizer, or as part of a dinner.

Note: This recipe makes a delicate, more elaborate deep-fried prawn than the usual. Try it!

*The batter is improved by using water chestnut powder (see Glossary), but if it is not available, use cornstarch instead.

**See Glossary.

CLAMS IN BLACK BEAN SAUCE
豉汁大蜆

2 lbs.	fresh clams in shells		¼ tsp.	salt
1½ tbsp.	salted black beans*		1 tsp.	dark soy sauce
2 tsp.	finely chopped garlic		1 tsp.	oyster sauce
1½ tbsp.	oil			
1 tbsp.	white wine			
¼ cup	chicken stock			
1½ tsp.	sugar			

THICKENING MIXTURE

1½ tsp. cornstarch mixed well with
3 tsp. cold water

1. Wash clams thoroughly. Drain.

2. Wash black beans twice. Drain. Mash into a paste with butt of a cleaver. Add chopped garlic.

3. Heat wok. Add oil, black bean mixture, and clams. Stir-fry for 2 minutes over high heat.

4. Sprinkle on the white wine, chicken stock, sugar, salt, dark soy sauce, and oyster sauce. Bring to a fast boil. Cover and cook for 7 minutes over high heat. (By now clams should be open. If not, cook a little longer.)

5. Stir in thickening mixture. Cook for 30 seconds. Serve.

Advance preparation: This recipe may be cooked a few hours in advance and kept at room temperature. Reheat for 2 minutes just before serving.

Serving suggestion: Serve with Bean Sprouts with Snow Peas, Curry Beef, and Steamed Rice.

Note: Clams cooked in this manner are quite different from the usual steamed clams. They are delicious!

*See Glossary, page 185.

CLAMS IN GARLIC SAUCE
薑葱大蜆

2 lbs.	fresh clams in shells		1	green onion, finely chopped
1 tbsp.	fermented bean cake*		1 tbsp.	white wine
1½ tsp.	sugar		¼ cup	chicken stock
1 tsp.	dark soy sauce			
1 tsp.	oyster sauce			
1 tbsp.	oil			
2 tsp.	finely chopped garlic			

THICKENING MIXTURE

1½ tsp.	cornstarch mixed well with
3 tsp.	cold water

1. Wash clams thoroughly and drain.

2. Mash bean cake into a paste. Add sugar, dark soy sauce, and oyster sauce.

3. Heat wok. Add oil, garlic, green onion, and clams. Stir-fry for 2 minutes over high heat.

4. Add bean cake mixture. Toss well. Add wine and chicken stock. Bring to a fast boil, cover, and cook for 7 minutes over high heat. (By now, clams should be open. If not, cook a little longer.)

5. Stir in thickening mixture. Cook for 30 seconds. Serve.

Advance preparation: This recipe may be cooked a few hours in advance and kept at room temperature. Reheat for 2 minutes just before serving.

Serving suggestion: Serve with Pot Stickers, Szechuan Spiced Chicken, and Steamed Rice.

*Fermented bean cakes are called furu and are sold in jars. See Glossary, page 183.

DEEP-FRIED SQUID
炸魷魚

Serves 4

		SEASONING MIXTURE	
1½ lb.	raw squid	¼ tsp.	salt
2 cups	oil	¼ tsp.	sugar
1 cup	tapioca starch* or cornstarch	1 tsp.	thin soy sauce
		1 tsp.	white wine
		Dash	pepper

1. Clean and wash squid. Drain. Pat dry with paper towel. Cut into 1½-inch pieces, leaving tentacles whole. (See "How to Clean a Squid," p. 12.)

2. Add seasoning mixture to squid and mix well.

3. Heat oil to 325°. Coat squid thoroughly, using 1 cup tapioca starch or cornstarch. Drop one half of squid into hot oil. Deep-fry for 3 minutes. Remove and drain on paper towels. Repeat procedure with remaining squid.

Condiments: Serve with catsup and Hot Mustard, page 53.

Advance preparation: Step 1 may be completed the night before and squid refrigerated. Pat squid dry again before using.

Serving suggestion: Serve as an appetizer, or as a course for lunch or dinner.

*See Glossary.

KUNG PAO PRAWNS
宮保蝦

½ lb.	raw prawns in shells
2 cups	oil for deep-frying
½ cup	raw skinned peanuts
½ lb.	broccoli
1 stalk	celery
1 can	baby corn ears* ("mini-corn")
2 tbsp.	oil for stir-frying
7	water chestnuts, thinly sliced (trimmed and peeled if fresh)
¼ tsp.	salt
¼ tsp.	sugar
1½ tsp.	finely chopped garlic
3 whole	dried red chili peppers
½ tbsp.	hoisin sauce
⅓ cup	chicken stock
1	green onion, slivered

SEASONING

¼ tsp.	salt
¼ tsp.	sugar
1½ tsp.	white wine
1½ tsp.	cornstarch
Dash	pepper

SAUCE

2 tsp.	Japanese rice vinegar mixed well with
1½ tsp.	thin soy sauce
1½ tsp.	sugar
1½ tsp.	sesame oil

THICKENING MIXTURE

1 tsp.	cornstarch mixed well with
2 tsp.	cold water

1. Shell, devein, wash, and drain prawns. Cut each prawn in half lengthwise.

2. Sprinkle seasoning on prawns and mix well.

3. In 2-quart saucepan heat 2 cups oil to 325°. Deep-fry raw peanuts until golden brown (about 3 minutes). Remove and drain on a paper towel. Set aside.

4. Peel off outer covering from broccoli stems. Cut stems and flowerettes diagonally into thin slices.

5. Remove celery strings with a vegetable peeler. Cut celery into 1½-inch pieces, then cut each lengthwise into strips, julienne style.

6. Cut baby corn diagonally into ¾-inch pieces.

7. Heat wok. Add 1 tbsp. oil, water chestnuts, broccoli, celery, and corn. Stir-fry for 2 minutes over high heat, sprinkling with ¼ tsp. salt and ¼ tsp. sugar. Remove from wok and set aside.

8. Heat wok. Add 1 tbsp. oil, chopped garlic, whole chili peppers, and prawns. Stir-fry for 2 minutes over high heat.

9. Add hoisin sauce and stir well, then add chicken stock. Cook, uncovered, for 2 minutes. Remove and discard chili peppers (or leave them in, if you prefer).

10. Add cooked water chestnut mixture and green onion. Mix well.

11. Stir in thickening mixture. Cook for 30 seconds.

12. Add sauce and mix well.

13. Add deep-fried peanuts. Mix well and serve.

Advance preparation: Steps 1 through 9 and the sauce may be prepared a few hours in advance and kept at room temperature.

Serving suggestion: Serve with Parchment Beef, Sweet and Sour Pork Chops, and Steamed Rice.

Variations: You may substitute snow peas or green bell pepper for broccoli, using the same cooking time. You may use ½ cup sliced bamboo shoots or jicama in place of water chestnuts.

*See Glossary, page 186.

MINCED OYSTERS WITH LETTUCE LEAVES
蠔豉鬆

Serves 8

1 head	iceberg lettuce, washed and drained until dry
¼ lb.	lean ground pork*
4	dried oysters**
10	small Chinese mushrooms (dried)
2¼ cups	warm water
8	dried shrimp*
4	water chestnuts (fresh or canned) or
	¼ cup finely chopped jicama
¼ lb.	raw prawns in shells (optional)
1½ tbsp.	oil
¼ cup	chicken stock
¼ lb.	Chinese Barbecued Pork, page 110, finely
	chopped
1	green onion, finely chopped

SEASONING

¼ tsp.	salt
¼ tsp.	sugar
½ tsp.	thin soy sauce
1 tsp.	cornstarch

THICKENING MIXTURE

2½ tsp.	cornstarch mixed well with
¼ cup	chicken stock
1 tsp.	dark soy sauce
½ tsp.	sugar
2 tsp.	white wine
1 tsp.	oyster sauce
1 tsp.	sesame oil
Dash	pepper

1. Carefully break off 8 outside leaves of lettuce, keeping them as whole as possible. Place on a serving platter.

2. Sprinkle seasoning on ground pork and mix well.

3. Soak dried oysters and mushrooms in 1 cup warm water for 20 minutes. Rinse and drain. Remove and discard mushroom stems. Chop mushrooms fine. Bring 1 cup water to a boil. Add dried oysters. Cover and cook for 10 minutes. Rinse and drain. Chop fine.

4. Soak dried shrimp for 5 minutes in ¼ cup warm water. Rinse, drain, and chop fine.

5. Peel fresh water chestnuts. Cut off tops and bottoms, and discard (canned are ready to use). Chop fine. If using jicama, peel and chop fine.

6. Shell, devein, wash, and drain prawns. Cut into very small pieces.

7. Heat wok. Add oil, ground pork, mushrooms, and dried shrimp. Stir-fry for 2 minutes over high heat. Add ¼ cup chicken stock. Bring to a fast boil, cover, and cook for 2 minutes.

8. Add oysters, prawns, barbecued pork, green onion, and water chestnuts or jicama. Mix thoroughly.

9. Stir in thickening mixture. Cook for 1 minute. Remove to a serving platter. To eat, place 2 tbsp. meat mixture on center of a lettuce leaf. Roll up and eat like a taco.

Advance preparation: Steps 1 through 7 and thickening mixture may be done a few hours ahead. Reheat to a boil before proceeding to steps 8 and 9.

Serving suggestion: This dish may be served as a first course, or served with Mandarin Chow Mein, Bean Sprouts with Snow Peas, and Steamed Rice.

Note: This dish is delicious and fun to eat, but the ingredients are expensive and require a lot of chopping. A food processor saves a great deal of time.

*See Glossary.

**Dried oysters usually come in cellophane packages, often unlabeled. See Glossary. They can be omitted if you are not fond of the oyster flavor. The dish tastes fine without them.

PRAWNS A LA SZECHUAN
乾燒明蝦

½ lb.	medium-sized raw prawns
1½ tbsp.	oil
¼ tsp.	salt
4 whole	dried red chili peppers
1½ tsp.	finely chopped garlic
1 tsp.	finely chopped ginger
1	green onion, finely chopped

SAUCE

1¼ tsp.	cornstarch
¼ cup	chicken stock
1 tbsp.	white wine
2 tsp.	hoisin sauce
1 tbsp.	catsup
1 tbsp.	sesame oil
1 tsp.	oyster sauce
½ tsp.	thin soy sauce
1 tsp.	sugar

1. Shell, devein, wash, and drain prawns.

2. To prepare sauce, add cornstarch to chicken stock, then add remaining ingredients for sauce. Mix well. Set aside.

3. Heat wok. Add oil, whole chili peppers, garlic, ginger, and green onion. Stir-fry for 30 seconds over high heat.

4. Add prawns. Stir-fry for 2 minutes over high heat. Sprinkle ¼ tsp. salt over prawns.

5. Add sauce from step 2. Bring to a fast boil. Cook, uncovered, for 30 seconds over high heat. Remove and discard chili peppers, or leave in, if you prefer. Serve.

Advance preparation: Steps 1 and 2 may be done a few hours in advance and kept at room temperature.

Serving suggestions: Serve with Mo Shu Pork with Mandarin Pancakes, Pot Stickers, and Steamed Rice.

PRAWNS WITH LOBSTER SAUCE
蝦球龍蝦糊

1 lb.	medium-sized raw prawns in shells
⅓ lb.	lean ground pork*
1½ tbsp.	salted black beans**
2½ tbsp.	oil
⅓ cup	chicken stock
2 tsp.	finely chopped garlic
½ cup	diced yellow onion
1 tbsp.	white wine
¾ cup	chicken stock
1	green onion, diced
⅓ cup	frozen peas, defrosted (optional)
2 tsp.	oyster sauce
2	eggs, beaten with a fork
2 tsp.	sesame oil

SEASONING FOR PRAWNS

½ tsp.	salt
1 tsp.	sugar
2 tsp.	cornstarch
Dash	pepper

SEASONING FOR GROUND PORK

½ tsp.	salt
½ tsp.	sugar
½ tsp.	thin soy sauce
1 tsp.	oyster sauce
2 tsp.	cornstarch
Dash	pepper

1. Shell, devein, wash, and drain prawns.

2. Sprinkle seasoning on prawns and mix well.

3. Sprinkle seasoning on ground pork and mix well.

4. Wash black beans twice and drain. Mash into a paste with butt of a cleaver.

5. Heat wok. Add 1 tbsp. oil and seasoned pork. Stir-fry for 2 minutes over high heat. Add ⅓ cup chicken stock. Cover and cook 3 minutes over high heat. Remove from wok and set aside.

6. Heat wok. Add 1½ tbsp. oil, chopped garlic, mashed black beans, diced yellow onion, and prawns. Stir-fry for 2 minutes over high heat.

(continued)

7. Add wine, ¾ cup chicken stock, green onion, frozen peas, and oyster sauce. Quickly bring to a boil and cook for 1 minute, uncovered, over high heat.

8. Add cooked ground pork. Mix well.

9. Add beaten egg and cook for 30 seconds.

10. Add sesame oil and mix well. Serve.

Advance preparation: Steps 1 through 8 may be done a few hours ahead and kept at room temperature.

Serving suggestion: Serve with Steak Cubes Chinese Style, West Lake Minced Beef Soup, and Steamed Rice.

Variations: Filet of sole or red snapper may be substituted for prawns, using same cooking time.

*See Glossary.

**See Glossary, page 185.

PRAWNS WITH SNOW PEAS
蘭豆炒蝦

Serves 4

½ lb.	medium-sized raw prawns in shells
¼ lb.	snow peas
1½ tbsp.	oil

SEASONING

¼ tsp.	salt
¼ tsp.	sugar
½ tsp.	thin soy sauce
¾ tsp.	cornstarch
Dash	pepper

THICKENING MIXTURE

1 tsp.	cornstarch mixed well with
¼ cup	chicken stock
1 tsp.	dark soy sauce
2 tsp.	white wine

1. Shell, devein, wash, and drain prawns.

2. Sprinkle seasoning on prawns and mix well.

3. Remove tips from snow peas and cut peas in half diagonally.

4. Heat wok. Add oil, prawns, and snow peas. Stir-fry for 1½ minutes over high heat.

5. Stir in thickening mixture. Cook for 1 minute. Serve.

Advance preparation: Steps 1 through 3 and thickening mixture may be done a few hours in advance. Keep at room temperature.

Serving suggestion: Serve with War Won Ton Soup, Chicken with Chili Peppers, and Steamed Rice.

SALT BAKED PRAWNS
椒鹽大蝦

Serves 4

FLAVORED SALT

2 tbsp.	salt
⅛ tsp.	five-spice powder

¾ lb.   medium-sized raw prawns in shells

2 tbsp.	cornstarch
4 tbsp.	oil
2 cloves	garlic, crushed
¾ tsp.	flavored salt
Dash	pepper

1. To make flavored salt, heat salt in dry frying pan (no oil) over medium heat for 2 minutes. Remove from heat and stir in five-spice powder. Mix well. Store extra flavored salt in an airtight container; it will keep indefinitely.

2. Using scissors, devein prawns without removing shells; slit shell along back of prawn just enough to allow removal of vein. Wash and drain. (Leaving shells on keeps them tender and juicy.)

3. Coat prawns with cornstarch (it is important that this be done just before cooking).

4. Heat wok or frying pan. Add oil and crushed garlic. Cook over medium heat for 30 seconds.

5. Add prawns. Pan-fry over medium heat for 2 minutes on each side (total cooking time 4 minutes).

6. Remove garlic and discard. Sprinkle ¾ tsp. flavored salt and dash pepper over prawns. Serve immediately.

(continued)

Advance preparation: Step 1 may be done a month ahead. Step 2 may be done a few hours in advance and refrigerated.

Serving suggestion: Serve with Sweet Rice Rolls and Chicken and Mushroom Rice Casserole.

Note: This is a favorite recipe in Chinese homes and is also available in some restaurants. It is called Salt-baked Prawns, even though the prawns are not baked.

WHOLE FRESH CRAB IN BLACK BEAN SAUCE
豉汁大蟹

Serves 4

1½–2 lb.	fresh whole crab (raw)
1½ tbsp.	salted black beans*
2 tsp.	finely chopped garlic
1 tsp.	finely chopped ginger
1	green onion, finely chopped
2 tbsp.	oil
1 tbsp.	white wine
1 tsp.	sugar

1 tsp.	thin soy sauce
1 tsp.	dark soy sauce
1 tbsp.	oyster sauce
Dash	pepper
1 cup	chicken stock

THICKENING MIXTURE

1½ tsp.	cornstarch mixed well with
3 tsp.	cold water

1. Prepare crab for cooking (see page 13).

2. Wash black beans twice, drain, and mash into a paste with butt of a cleaver. Add chopped garlic, ginger, and green onion.

3. Heat wok and add oil and black bean sauce mixture. Stir-fry for 30 seconds over high heat. Add crab and stir-fry for 3 minutes over high heat.

4. Sprinkle evenly over top: wine, sugar, thin soy sauce, dark soy sauce, oyster sauce, and dash pepper. Toss well.

5. Add chicken stock. Bring to a fast boil over high heat. Cover and cook for 5 minutes (crab shell should turn a nice red color).

6. Stir in thickening mixture. Cook 30 seconds. Serve.

Advance preparation: Steps 1 and 2 and thickening mixture may be prepared a few hours in advance. Refrigerate crab. The rest can stand at room temperature.

Serving suggestion: Serve with Bean Cake Soup, Vegetables De Luxe, and Steamed Rice.

Note: When crab is prepared this way, it has a deliciously different flavor from the usual boiled crab.

*"Salty Black Beans," which come in a soft package or box. See Glossary, page 185.

WHOLE FRESH CRAB IN CURRY SAUCE
咖喱大蟹

Serves 4

1½–2lb.	fresh whole crab (raw)
2 tbsp.	oil
1 tsp.	finely chopped garlic
¼ cup	chopped yellow onion
2	green onions, sliced into ½-inch lengths
¼ tsp.	salt
2 tsp.	sugar

1½ tsp.	thin soy sauce
1 tbsp.	white wine
1¼ tbsp.	curry powder
1 cup	chicken stock

THICKENING MIXTURE

2 tsp.	cornstarch mixed well with
1 tbsp.	cold water

1. Prepare crab for cooking (see page 13).

2. Heat wok. Add oil and garlic. Stir-fry for 30 seconds over high heat. Add yellow onion, green onions, and crab. Stir-fry for 3 minutes.

3. Sprinkle evenly over top: salt, sugar, thin soy sauce, wine, and curry powder. Toss well.

4. Add chicken stock. Bring to a fast boil over high heat, cover, and cook for 5 minutes (crab shell should turn a nice red color).

5. Stir in thickening mixture. Cook for 30 seconds. Serve.

(continued)

Advance preparation: You may complete step 1 and prepare green and yellow onions, garlic, and thickening mixture a few hours in advance. Refrigerate crab. The rest can stand at room temperature.

Serving suggestion: Serve with Beef with Green Beans, Stuffed Bell Pepper, and Steamed Rice.

WHOLE FRESH CRAB IN EGG SAUCE
芙蓉大蟹

Serves 4

1½–2 lb.	fresh whole crab (raw)
2 oz.	lean ground pork*
2 tbsp.	oil
1	green onion, diced
1 tsp.	finely chopped ginger
¼ cup	finely chopped yellow onion
½ tsp.	salt
½ tsp.	sugar
1 tbsp.	white wine
1 tsp.	thin soy sauce

¾ tbsp.	oyster sauce
Dash	pepper
1 cup	chicken stock
1 large	egg, lightly beaten with a fork

SEASONING

⅛ tsp.	salt
⅛ tsp.	sugar
¼ tsp.	thin soy sauce
1 tsp.	cornstarch

1. Prepare crab for cooking (see page 13).

2. Sprinkle seasoning on ground pork and mix well.

3. Heat wok. Add oil, green onion, ginger, yellow onion, and ground pork. Stir-fry for 1 minute over high heat.

4. Add crab pieces to mixture. Stir-fry for 2 minutes over high heat.

5. Add salt, sugar, wine, thin soy sauce, oyster sauce, and dash pepper. Toss well.

6. Add chicken stock. Bring to a fast boil over high heat. Cover and cook for 5 minutes (crab shell should turn a nice red color).

150

7. Add beaten egg and cook for 30 seconds. Do not overcook! Serve.

Advance preparation: Steps 1 and 2 may be done ahead and refrigerated.

Serving suggestion: Serve with Asparagus in Oyster Sauce, Kung Pao Chicken, and Steamed Rice.

Note: Fresh crab prepared this way is truly delicious!

*See Glossary.

WHOLE FRESH CRAB WITH GINGER AND SCALLIONS
羌葱大蟹

Serves 4

1½–2 lb.	fresh whole crab (raw)	½ tsp.	salt
3	green onions	1 tsp.	sugar
3 tbsp.	oil	2 tsp.	thin soy sauce
1 slice	ginger (1½-inch diameter) ½ inch thick, crushed	2 tsp.	oyster sauce
2 tbsp.	cornstarch	Dash	pepper
2 tbsp.	white wine	¼ cup	chicken stock

1. Prepare crab for cooking (see page 13).

2. Cut green onions into 1-inch pieces.

3. Heat wok. Add oil, ginger, and green onions. Stir-fry for 30 seconds over high heat.

4. Coat each piece of crab lightly with cornstarch (it is important that this be done just before cooking!). Drop into hot oil. Pan-fry for 30 seconds on each side, over high heat.

5. Sprinkle evenly over top: wine, salt, sugar, thin soy sauce, oyster sauce, and dash pepper. Toss well.

6. Add chicken stock. Bring to a fast boil over high heat. Cover and cook for 5 minutes (crab shell should turn a nice red color). Serve.

(continued)

Advance preparation: Steps 1 and 2 may be done ahead and refrigerated.

Serving suggestion: Serve with Steamed Spareribs with Black Bean Sauce, Beef under Snow, and Steamed Rice.

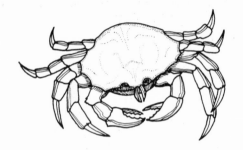

VEGETABLES

ASPARAGUS IN BLACK BEAN SAUCE
豉汁梨筍

Serves 4

1¼ lb.	fresh asparagus (about 4 cups cut up)
1½ tbsp.	salted black beans*
1½ tsp.	finely chopped garlic
½ tsp.	crushed dried red pepper**
2 tbsp.	oil
¾ tsp.	salt
1 tsp.	sugar
1 tbsp.	white wine

¾ cup	chicken stock
1	green onion, finely chopped

THICKENING MIXTURE

2 tsp.	cornstarch mixed well with
1 tbsp.	cold water
1 tsp.	dark soy sauce
2 tsp.	oyster sauce
2 tsp.	sesame oil

1. Break off and discard tough base-ends of asparagus. Cut each spear diagonally into ½-inch slices (each slice should be about 1½ inches long).

2. Rinse black beans twice. Drain. Mash into a paste with butt of a cleaver. Add chopped garlic and crushed red pepper.

3. Heat wok. Add oil, black bean mixture, and asparagus. Stir-fry for 2 minutes over medium-high heat. Add salt, sugar, and white wine. Mix well. Add chicken stock. Bring to a fast boil and cook for 2 minutes, uncovered, over high heat.

4. Stir in thickening mixture. Cook for 30 seconds. Remove to a serving platter. Sprinkle chopped green onion over top. Serve immediately.

Advance preparation: Steps 1 and 2 may be done a few hours in advance.

(continued)

*"Salty Black Beans," which usually come in a soft package. See Glossary, page 185.

**Omit crushed red pepper if you prefer a less spicy dish.

ASPARAGUS IN OYSTER SAUCE
蠔油梨筍

Serves 4

1½ lb.	fresh asparagus (about 4 cups cut up)	1 qt.	water
3½ tbsp.	oil	2 tbsp.	oyster sauce

1. Break off and discard tough base-ends of asparagus. Cut each spear diagonally into ½-inch slices (each slice should be about 1½ inches long).

2. Place 3½ tbsp. oil in a small saucepan. Set aside.

3. Bring 1 qt. water to a boil and add asparagus. Cook uncovered for 2 minutes over high heat. (Start timing immediately. Do not wait for water to return to a boil.) Drain.

4. While asparagus is draining, heat oil for 1 minute over high heat. Place asparagus in a shallow dish and immediately pour hot oil over it. (Oil should be so hot that it sizzles when poured over vegetable.)

5. Pour oyster sauce over asparagus. Mix well. Serve immediately.

Advance preparation: Steps 1 and 2 may be done a few hours in advance.

Note: Asparagus prepared this way is delicious; it is one of my family's favorites. It is also very quick. Do try it!

Variation: Bok choy, Swiss chard, zucchini, cabbage, Napa cabbage, broccoli, and Chinese broccoli can all be prepared in this manner, using the same cooking time.

154

BEAN CAKE WITH GROUND PORK
麻婆豆腐

2 pieces	dried black fungus* *or*
	½ cup sliced fresh mushrooms
1 cup	warm water
½ lb.	lean ground pork*
1 pkg.	fresh bean cake (tofu)**
2 tbsp.	hot bean sauce* (Szechuan style)
2 tsp.	sugar
3 tbsp.	oil
⅓ cup	chicken stock
1½ qt.	water
2 tsp.	finely chopped garlic
½ tsp.	salt
½ cup	shredded bamboo shoots***
½ cup	frozen peas, defrosted
¾ cup	chicken stock

1 tbsp.	oyster sauce
1½ tbsp.	sesame oil
2	green onions, finely chopped

SEASONING

¾ tsp.	salt
¾ tsp.	sugar
¾ tsp.	thin soy sauce
2 tsp.	white wine
2 tsp.	cornstarch
Dash	pepper

THICKENING MIXTURE

1 tbsp.	cornstarch mixed well with
2 tbsp.	cold water
1 tsp.	dark soy sauce

1. Soak black fungus for 15 minutes in 1 cup warm water. Rinse, drain. Remove and discard stems. Cut fungus into small pieces.

2. Sprinkle seasoning on ground pork and mix well.

3. Cut bean cake into ¼-inch cubes.

4. Mash hot bean sauce into a paste, then add 2 tsp. sugar. Set aside.

5. Heat wok, add 1 tbsp. oil, and stir-fry ground pork for 2 minutes.

6. Add ⅓ cup chicken stock. Cover and cook for 3 minutes over high heat. Remove from wok and set aside.

(continued)

7. Bring 1½ qt. water to a boil. Add diced bean cake. Boil for 30 seconds, uncovered. Remove and drain.

8. Immediately heat wok and add 2 tbsp. oil, chopped garlic, bean sauce mixture, and bean cake. Stir-fry for 1 minute over high heat. Sprinkle ½ tsp. salt over bean cake. Add bamboo shoots, black fungus or mushrooms, peas, and ¾ cup chicken stock. Bring to a fast boil and cook uncovered for 1 minute.

9. Add cooked ground pork, oyster sauce, sesame oil, and green onions. Toss well.

10. Stir in thickening mixture, cook for 30 seconds, and serve.

Advance preparation: Steps 1 through 6 may be prepared a few hours in advance. Keep at room temperature until ready to complete the recipe.

Serving suggestion: Serve with Steak Cubes Chinese Style, Spring Rolls, and Steamed Rice.

*See Glossary.

**Buy firm bean cake for cooking. It comes in a package of 2 or 4 pieces. See Glossary.

***Buy winter bamboo shoots if possible. See Glossary.

BEAN SPROUTS WITH SNOW PEAS
芽菜蘭豆

1 lb.   bean sprouts
¼ lb.   snow peas
1 tbsp.   raw sesame seeds (optional)
1½ tbsp.   oil
½ tsp.   salt
½ tsp.   sugar
⅓ cup   chicken stock
½ tbsp.   sesame oil

THICKENING MIXTURE

2½ tsp.   cornstarch mixed well with
1 tbsp.   cold water
2 tsp.   dark soy sauce
2 tsp.   white wine
1½ tsp.   oyster sauce

1. Wash and drain bean sprouts.

2. Remove tips from snow peas and cut peas diagonally into pieces ¼ inch wide.

3. Toast sesame seeds by heating in a dry frying pan over medium-low heat until golden brown, stirring occasionally to keep them from burning (about 3 minutes).

4. Combine ingredients for thickening mixture. Set aside.

5. Heat wok. Add oil. Stir-fry bean sprouts and snow peas for 1½ minutes over high heat. Add salt, sugar, and chicken stock. Bring to a fast boil, uncovered.

6. Stir in thickening mixture. Cook for 30 seconds.

7. Add sesame oil. Mix well. Remove to serving platter.

8. Sprinkle sesame seeds over top. Serve.

Advance preparation: Step 3 can be done several days ahead. Store sesame seeds in a covered container at room temperature. Steps 1, 2, and 4 may be done, and the mixture made, several hours ahead. Keep at room temperature.

Serving suggestion: This recipe goes well with almost any dish you might serve.

BLACK AND STRAW MUSHROOMS IN OYSTER SAUCE
蠔油雙菇

Serves 6

3 oz.	dried Chinese mushrooms (about 40 small size)		4 cups	chicken stock
1 tbsp.	cornstarch		15 oz.	can peeled straw mushrooms,* rinsed and drained
2	green onions		2½ tbsp.	oyster sauce
1 tbsp.	oil		1 tbsp.	dark soy sauce
1 slice	ginger (1¼-inch diameter) 1 inch thick, peeled and crushed			
¼ tsp.	salt			
1 tbsp.	white wine			
1 tsp.	sugar			

THICKENING MIXTURE

1½ tbsp.	cornstarch mixed well with
3 tbsp.	cold water
1 tsp.	sugar

1. Soak dried Chinese mushrooms in warm water to cover for 30 minutes. Rinse, squeeze dry. Remove and discard stems. Leave mushrooms whole. Add cornstarch and mix well.

2. Cut off green onion tops. Leave whole for cooking. Sliver white bottom parts and reserve for garnish.

3. Heat wok. Add 1 tbsp. oil and Chinese mushrooms. Stir-fry for 2 minutes over high heat. Add green onion tops, ginger, salt, white wine, sugar, and chicken stock. Bring to a quick boil. Reduce heat to medium low. Cover and cook 1 hour, stirring occasionally to be sure there is sufficient liquid. There should be 2 cups liquid remaining. If not, add sufficient chicken stock to make 2 cups. Remove and discard green onion tops and ginger.

4. Add straw mushrooms, oyster sauce, and dark soy sauce. Cook for 5 minutes over high heat.

5. Stir in thickening mixture. Cook for 30 seconds over high heat.

6. Remove to a serving platter. Garnish with slivered green onions and serve.

Advance preparation: Steps 1–4 may be done several days in advance and refrigerated. Reheat by simmering for 5 minutes, then complete steps 5 and 6 immediately before serving.

158

Note: Chinese mushrooms make a very good "company" dish. The mushrooms are an expensive delicacy, and this method of preparation gives them the attention they deserve.

Serving suggestion: Serve with Sweet and Sour Pork Chops, Velvet Chicken, and Steamed Rice.

*See Glossary, page 190.

BROCCOLI IN OYSTER SAUCE
蠔油芥蘭

Serves 4

1 bunch broccoli (about 1 ¼ lb.)
3½ tbsp. oil

1½ qt. water
2½ tbsp. oyster sauce

1. Peel off tough outer covering from broccoli stems. Cut stems and flowerettes diagonally into 1½-inch pieces.

2. Place 3½ tbsp. oil in a small saucepan. Set aside.

3. Bring 1½ qt. water to a boil. Add broccoli and cook, uncovered, for 2 minutes over high heat. (Start timing immediately. Do not wait until water returns to a boil.) Drain.

4. While broccoli is draining, heat oil for 1 minute over high heat. Place broccoli in a shallow dish and immediately pour hot oil over it. (Oil should be so hot that it sizzles when poured over vegetable.)

5. Pour oyster sauce over broccoli. Mix well and serve immediately.

Advance preparation: Steps 1 and 2 may be done a few hours in advance. Keep at room temperature.

Variation: Try zucchini, Swiss chard, bok choy, asparagus, cabbage, or Napa cabbage prepared this way. They all require the same cooking time.

BROCCOLI WITH BARBECUED PORK
叉燒芥蘭

Serves 5

1 bunch   broccoli (about 1¼ lb.)
           (either Chinese or regular broccoli)
½ lb.   Chinese Barbecued Pork, page 110
1½ tbsp.   oil
½ tsp.   salt
1 tsp.   sugar
½ cup   chicken stock

THICKENING MIXTURE

2 tsp.   cornstarch mixed well with
1 tbsp.   cold water
1 tsp.   dark soy sauce
2 tsp.   oyster sauce
2 tsp.   white wine
2 tsp.   sesame oil

1. Peel off thick covering from broccoli stems. Cut stems and flowerettes diagonally into 1½-inch pieces. (If using Chinese broccoli, the leaves should be used also.)

2. Cut barbecued pork into thin slices about 1½-by-½ inch.

3. Heat wok. Add oil and broccoli. Stir-fry for 2 minutes over high heat. Sprinkle with ½ tsp. salt and 1 tsp. sugar. Add ½ cup chicken stock. Bring to a fast boil and cook uncovered for 2 minutes.

4. Add barbecued pork. Mix well.

5. Stir in thickening mixture. Cook for 30 seconds. Serve.

Advance preparation: Steps 1 and 2 may be completed the night before and refrigerated.

Serving suggestion: Serve with Fisherman's Soup and Shrimp Fried Rice.

Variation: Asparagus or bok choy may be used instead of broccoli, using the same cooking time.

CUCUMBER AND CHICKEN SALAD
黃瓜雞沙律

Serves 4

1	cucumber (about ½ lb.)	**SAUCE**	
⅛ tsp.	salt	½ tsp.	dry mustard
1	whole chicken breast (about 1 lb.)	1¼ tbsp.	Japanese rice vinegar
¼ tsp.	salt	1 tbsp.	sugar
1 cup	shredded iceberg lettuce	1 tsp.	thin soy sauce
		½ tsp.	chili paste with garlic*
		2 tsp.	oyster sauce
		1 tbsp.	sesame oil

1. Cut cucumber lengthwise. Scrape out seeds. Cut cucumber diagonally into very thin slices (less than ¼ inch thick). Place in a colander. Sprinkle with ⅛ tsp. salt. Let stand for 40 minutes. Squeeze out excess liquid. (This helps remove any bitterness.) Set aside.

2. Place whole chicken breast on a plate. Sprinkle with ¼ tsp. salt. Steam for 20 minutes (see "Steaming," page 7). Let cool. When cool, remove skin and bones and discard. Shred chicken meat by hand into ¼-inch strips, julienne style.

3. Place cucumbers and chicken in a mixing bowl.

4. Combine ingredients for sauce. Mix well. Pour over chicken and cucumbers. Toss well. Refrigerate for 2 hours or more. Before serving, add shredded lettuce. Toss thoroughly. Place on a platter and serve.

Serving suggestion: Goes well with almost any dish and is ideal for hot weather.

*See Glossary.

161

EGGPLANT SZECHUAN STYLE
四川茄子

2	Oriental eggplants* (½ lb.)	
	or ½ lb. eggplant	
¾ tbsp.	hot bean sauce**	
1½ tbsp.	oil	
¾ tsp.	finely chopped garlic	
¾ tsp.	finely chopped ginger	
1	green onion, finely chopped	
½ tbsp.	sesame oil	

(handwritten note: mix, set aside)

SAUCE

½ cup	chicken stock
¼ tsp.	salt
2 tsp.	sugar
2 tsp.	white wine
1 tsp.	dark soy sauce
1 tsp.	oyster sauce
2 tsp.	Japanese rice vinegar or cider vinegar

(handwritten note: mix, set aside)

THICKENING MIXTURE

½ tsp.	cornstarch mixed well with
1 tsp.	cold water

1. Cut off and discard tips of eggplant. Cut Oriental eggplant diagonally into slices about ¼ inch thick. (If using eggplant, cut into quarters, then cut diagonally into slices about ¼ inch thick.)

2. Mash bean sauce into a paste with handle of a cleaver.

3. Mix together ingredients for sauce. Set aside.

4. Heat wok. Add oil, garlic, and ginger. Stir-fry for 30 seconds over high heat. Add hot bean sauce and eggplant. Stir-fry for 30 seconds over high heat.

5. Add sauce. Cover and cook for 3 minutes over high heat.

6. Stir in thickening mixture. Cook for 30 seconds over high heat.

7. Add chopped green onion and sesame oil. Mix well and serve.

Advance preparation: Steps 1 through 3 may be done a day ahead and refrigerated.

Serving suggestion: This may be served as a vegetable dish with any meat or seafood dish.

*Oriental eggplant is found at some supermarkets or any Oriental market. It is long and slender and is more tender than the globe-shaped variety. See Glossary, page 188.

**If you prefer a less spicy dish, use Cantonese-style bean sauce. See Glossary.

JAI
羅漢齋

Serves 8

20	pieces dried bamboo shoot tips*	5 cups	chicken stock
	warm water for soaking	1¾ tbsp.	wet bean curd*
1 qt.	water for boiling	4 cups	Napa cabbage, cut into 1-inch pieces
30 small	Chinese mushrooms (dried)		
30	pieces lily flowers*	**SEASONING**	
8	dried oysters, left whole* (optional)	2 tbsp.	white wine
8	pieces dried black fungus*	1 tbsp.	dark soy sauce
20	dried sweet bean curds*	2 tsp.	thin soy sauce
4 oz.	pkg. bean threads*	1½ tbsp.	oyster sauce
4	dried red dates*	¼ tsp.	salt
1 tbsp.	oil	1 tbsp.	sugar

1. Most of the ingredients for jai are preserved by drying, and they must be reconstituted by soaking in water. Using hot or warm water speeds process. Soak dried bamboo shoot tips in 1 qt. warm water for 2 days, changing water daily. Bring to a boil 1 qt. water over high heat. Reduce heat to medium and add bamboo shoot tips. Cover and cook for 1 hour. (Check water level occasionally.) Drain off and discard liquid.

2. Soak Chinese mushrooms, lily flowers, dried oysters, and dried black fungus in 1 qt. warm water for 20 minutes. Rinse and drain. Cut off and discard mushroom stems. Cut ¼ inch off pointed end of lily flowers and discard. Remove and discard stems from black fungus. Cut black fungus into ½-inch strips.

3. In a separate container, soak the dried sweet bean curd for 15 minutes in 2 cups warm water. Rinse, drain, and cut into 1½-inch pieces.

(continued)

163

4. In a separate container, soak bean threads in warm water for 10 minutes. Rinse and drain. Cut twice with scissors (for easier eating).

5. Rinse red dates and cut in half. Discard seeds.

6. Heat wok and add oil, mushrooms, and bamboo shoots. Stir-fry for 2 minutes over high heat. Add chicken stock and red dates. Cover and cook over medium heat for 30 minutes.

7. Add wet bean curd, lily flowers, black fungus, sweet bean curd, and oysters. Mix well.

8. Add seasoning mixture. Cover and cook for 15 minutes over medium-high heat.

9. Add bean threads and Napa cabbage. Cover and cook for 5 minutes over high heat. Serve.

Advance preparation: You may complete recipe a few days in advance and refrigerate. Flavor actually improves the second day.

Serving suggestion: Serve with Stewed Chicken and Steamed Rice.

Note: Jai is the traditional dish every household cooks for Chinese New Year. An all-vegetable dish containing 10 or more vegetarian ingredients, Jai is also known as the "Monk's dish." Buddhist monks, out of reverence for all forms of animal life, will eat only a vegetarian diet. Thus, Chinese households celebrate the New Year and the reverence of life in the Buddhist tradition by partaking of this dish.

*See Glossary.

LETTUCE IN OYSTER SAUCE
蠔油生菜
Serves 4

| 1 small | head iceberg lettuce (about 14 oz.) | 1 qt. | water |
| 3½ tbsp. | oil | 2½ tbsp. | oyster sauce |

1. Rinse, drain, and cut lettuce into 2-inch pieces.

2. Place 3½ tbsp. oil in a small saucepan. Set aside.

3. Bring 1 qt. water to a boil. Add lettuce. Cook uncovered for 1 minute over high heat. (Start timing immediately. Do not wait for water to boil.) Drain.

4. While lettuce is draining, heat oil for 1 minute over high heat. Place lettuce in a shallow dish. Immediately pour hot oil over it (oil should be so hot it sizzles when it hits vegetable).

5. Pour oyster sauce over lettuce, mix well, and serve immediately.

Advance preparation: Steps 1 and 2 may be done a few hours in advance.

Variations: Snow peas, bean sprouts, spinach, celery, and green bell peppers may also be prepared this way, using same cooking time.

Note: This is a quick and easy recipe, and delicious. It is well worth a try.

SZECHUAN-STYLE GREEN BEANS
四川豆角

Serves 4

12 oz.	green beans
1 qt.	water
2 cups	oil for deep-frying
2 tbsp.	raw cashew nuts or raw peanuts
	(roasted nuts may be substituted if desired)
1 tbsp.	hot bean sauce*
1½ tbsp.	oil for stir-frying
1½ tsp.	finely chopped garlic
½ tsp.	salt
1	green onion, finely chopped

SAUCE

⅓ cup	chicken stock mixed well with
1½ tsp.	sugar
2 tsp.	sesame oil
2 tsp.	Japanese rice vinegar
1 tsp.	oyster sauce
1 tsp.	dark soy sauce
2 tsp.	white wine

THICKENING MIXTURE

1 tsp.	cornstarch mixed well with
2 tsp.	cold water

1. Remove tips from green beans; cut beans diagonally into 1½-inch pieces.

(continued)

2. Bring 1 qt. water to a boil. Add green beans. Boil for 7 minutes, uncovered. Drain.

3. Heat 2 cups oil in a small saucepan to 300°. Deep-fry nuts until golden brown, approximately 3 minutes. (For convenience, fry nuts in a Chinese strainer.) Drain and chop fine.

4. Mash bean sauce into a paste with handle of a cleaver. Add sauce and mix well.

5. Heat wok. Add 1½ tbsp. oil, chopped garlic, and green beans. Stir-fry for 1½ minutes over high heat. Sprinkle with ½ tsp. salt and add sauce. Toss well.

6. Stir in thickening mixture. Cook for 30 seconds. Remove to a serving platter.

7. Sprinkle chopped green onion and chopped nuts over the top. Serve.

Advance preparation: Step 3 can be done several days ahead. Store deep-fried nuts in a covered container at room temperature. Steps 1, 2, and 4 can be done, and thickening mixture made, several hours ahead and kept at room temperature.

Note: A vegetarian favorite!

Variation: Asparagus or broccoli may be substituted for green beans. Omit parboiling. After adding sauce in step 5, bring to a fast boil and cook, uncovered, for 2 minutes.

*Szechuan bean sauce is very hot! Cantonese-style bean sauce may be substituted. See Glossary.

VEGETABLES DE LUXE
什錦瓜菜

Serves 4

1 whole	Chinese preserved radish*
	(½ cup soaked and sliced)
1 cup	warm water
2 pieces	dried black fungus**
	(½ cup soaked and sliced) *or*
	½ cup sliced fresh mushrooms
1 cup	warm water
2 stalks	celery
½	green bell pepper *or*
	15 snow peas
½ can	baby corn ears*** ("mini-corn")
1	carrot
2 tbsp.	oil

¾ tsp.	salt
1 tsp.	sugar
½ cup	chicken stock

THICKENING MIXTURE

1 tbsp.	cornstarch
1 tbsp.	cold water
1 tbsp.	dark soy sauce
1 tbsp.	white wine
2 tsp.	oyster sauce
2 tsp.	sesame oil
½ tsp.	sugar

1. Rinse Chinese preserved radish. Cut into thin strips julienne style. Soak in 1 cup warm water for 15 minutes. Rinse and drain.

2. Soak dried black fungus in 1 cup warm water for 10 minutes. Rinse and drain. Remove and discard stems. Cut fungus into thin strips, julienne style.

3. Peel strings from celery. Cut into 1½-inch pieces. Cut each piece lengthwise into ¼-inch strips, julienne style.

4. Remove seeds from bell pepper. Cut into ¼-inch strips. If using snow peas, remove tips. Cut diagonally into pieces approximately 1 inch wide.

5. Cut corn diagonally into ½-inch pieces.

6. Peel carrot. Cut diagonally into very thin slices.

7. Heat wok. Add oil and preserved radish, black fungus or fresh mushrooms, pepper or snow peas, celery, corn, and carrot. Stir-fry over high heat for 2 minutes.

(continued)

8. Add salt, sugar, and chicken stock. Bring quickly to a boil.

9. Stir in thickening mixture. Cook for 30 seconds. Serve.

Advance preparation: Steps 1 through 6 may be done day before and refrigerated until ready to cook.

Serving suggestion: Serve this dish with any meat or seafood dish.

*Chinese radish preserved with chili powder, salt, and spices. See Glossary, page 193.

**See Glossary, page 188.

***See Glossary, page 186.

NOODLES AND RICE

JENNIE'S NOODLE SOUP
什錦湯麵

2 qt.	water			
1 pkg.	(1 lb.) fresh Chinese noodles*		**THICKENING MIXTURE**	
1½ qt.	chicken stock		1 tbsp.	cornstarch mixed well with
1 tbsp.	oil		½ cup	chicken stock
½ cup	diced bamboo shoots**		1 tbsp.	dark soy sauce
1 cup	diced Chinese Barbecued Pork, page 110		1 tbsp.	sesame oil
1 cup	diced bok choy or broccoli		1 tbsp.	white wine
2	green onions, finely chopped		1 tsp.	sugar

1. Bring 2 qt. water to a boil. Add noodles and cook, uncovered, for 2 minutes. Pour into a colander and rinse with cold water. Drain and set aside.

2. Bring chicken stock to a boil. Meanwhile, heat wok. Add oil, bamboo shoots, barbecued pork, and bok choy or broccoli. Stir-fry for 2 minutes over high heat.

3. Add thickening mixture. Cook for 1 minute. Keep warm.

4. Add cooked noodles to boiling chicken stock. Cook for 1 minute. Pour into a large serving bowl. Top with barbecued pork and vegetable mixture and garnish with green onions. Serve.

Condiment: Each person is served with a small dish containing ½ tsp. Hot Oil (page 54) and 1 tsp. thin soy sauce.

Advance preparation: All vegetables may be chopped and step 1 completed the night before and refrigerated.

Serving suggestion: This soup may be served in 1 large serving bowl as described above, or in individual bowls with barbecued pork and vegetable topping, garnished with green onion.

(continued)

Note: All diced ingredients should be the same size, approximately ¼-inch cubes.

*See Glossary, page 191.

**If possible, buy winter bamboo shoots. If not available, use any good brand. See Glossary.

MANDARIN CHOW MEIN
北方色炒麵

Serves 8

2½ qt.	water	¾ lb.	bean sprouts, rinsed and drained
1 lb.	fresh Chinese noodles*	1	green onion, slivered
2 tbsp.	oil	¼ tsp.	salt
1½ tsp.	dark soy sauce	2 tsp.	oyster sauce
½ tsp.	salt (approximate)	1 tsp.	thin soy sauce

1	whole chicken breast *or*
	1 cup chicken meat
10	small Chinese mushrooms (dried) *or*
	1 cup sliced fresh mushrooms
1 cup	warm water
¼ lb.	Chinese Barbecued Pork, page 110
2 stalks	celery
1½ tbsp.	oil
1 cup	chicken stock

SEASONING

⅓ tsp.	salt
½ tsp.	sugar
½ tsp.	thin soy sauce
1 tsp.	oyster sauce
2 tsp.	white wine
2 tsp.	cornstarch
Dash	pepper

1. Bring 2½ qt. water to a boil. Divide noodles into 2 portions. Add 1 portion to boiling water and cook for 2 minutes.

2. While noodles are cooking, heat frying pan over high heat. (Frying pan must be hot so noodles will not stick, but not so hot that they will burn. Teflon frying pans are ideal.) Add 1 tbsp. oil. Reduce heat to medium high. Using a Chinese strainer, remove noodles from water, allow to drain slightly, and add to hot frying pan. Add ¾ tsp. dark soy sauce and mix thoroughly. Flatten noodles to cover bottom of frying pan. Pan-fry until golden brown (about 5 minutes), checking bottom of "pancake" periodically to avoid burning it.